Time and Human Language Now

Time and Human Language Now

Jonathan Boyarin and Martin Land

PRICKLY PARADIGM PRESS
CHICAGO

Prickly Paradigm Press, LLC
5629 South University Avenue
Chicago, Il 60637

www.prickly-paradigm.com

ISBN-10: 0-9794057-3-4
ISBN-13: 978-0-9794057-3-0
LCCN: 2008937606

Printed in the United States of America on acid-free paper.

thln_001 (Jonathan)

On 7/20/06, Jonathan Boyarin wrote:

No, this is not quite what Jonathan Boyarin wrote back on July 20, not quite. Now Jonathan is thinking of the beginning of a book, in the form of a record of correspondence (an epistolary scholarship?) that he and Martin Land will write together. And thus he bears in mind, as addressee, not only Martin, but you. He means for you not only to listen in on (or "read into") the correspondence, but also to... he wants to write, "understand," but he is not sure what that means and even worse, he fears it will sound imperious.

In what follows, think (if you will) of yourself as "Jonathan" when reading Martin's text, and as

"Martin" when reading Jonathan's. And we will try to think of you, as well as of each other, when we write. Some obscure references may still find their way into our text. We are a couple of old college friends carrying on a conversation that began in a coffee shop over thirty years ago, and we have more than once complained and delighted in the impression that no one else would likely understand what we say to each other. Such idiosyncrasy is not our goal.

Still, it is nice to be able to throw some Yiddish into an e-mail letter, so I wrote:

>*I was very briefly (for about 30 seconds) tremendously excited by a notion that passed through my head very early this morning. I was walking into* shul, *and the* gabbai *asked me if I would take the Torah out at the proper time (we're currently* davening *in a room other than where the Torah scrolls are kept). I said, "Sure, as long as I'm not* davening;" *and when he didn't quite catch my drift, clarified "as long as I'm not sent up to the* amud," *that is, told to lead the service as a mourner (which I was, in the end).*

"Shul," dear friend, is simply an old-fashioned word for synagogue, and this is indeed an old-fashioned synagogue. "Gabbai"—how do they translate it—here means the fellow who assigns roles to various participants in the course of the prayer service. "Davening" is a Yiddish word that means "praying," and it's interesting because not even the best Yiddish cultural historians know where it comes from. Here, I've used it twice, once to refer to what all the members of the congregation are doing together, and once to refer to actual leadership of the service. Being sent up to the "amud," or lectern, is a less ambiguous term for being instructed to lead that particular service.

For some reason (perhaps the early hour; I was neither entirely awake nor quite lucid), this mundane exchange led me to think of how astonishing it is that we communicate by language at all, and how absolutely fundamental communication in language is, first, to our sense of being human and, second, to our sense of being *per se*. And a title popped into my head: *Time and Human Language Now*.

It struck me that this is the kind of thing I could easily prepare a lecture on, but also the kind of broad theme I don't see myself meditating on for a whole book's worth. A topic can, of course, easily be too large to be the subject of an entire book.

But why should the choices be limited to writing more or fewer words all by myself? I knew almost instantly that I had another option. For Martin and I had recently had a satisfying, if not actually happy, experience writing together on a rather bleak subject— the second election of George W. Bush and the serious contemplation of human extinction portended by that event. Friends had asked whether we might collaborate again, and both of us knew we wanted to; but what do you say after you've said that the world is ending, and that repentance is just another avoidance mechanism? The answer (one answer) is: you seize the miracle of being able to talk, now, still, even if all you're talking about is a plausible fear of the ultimate silence. You talk about the astonishment of communication, of dialogue. You talk about how much we still have to lose.

I didn't, back on July 20, and now (on September 7, once again in Kansas) know how to artic-ulate the WHOLE THING any better than that. So I began, immediately, to break the topic into some possible component parts, some themes this correspondence about talking now might take up, and I set them down as a series of possible starters.

First, it was already clear that both tense and person would need careful attention in this exchange, which is fundamentally about tense and person. I thought I remembered a point made by the linguist Emile Benveniste: that the notion of any present, and the linguistic second person (the possibility of my addressing you) are mutually dependent concepts. That is not, it seems, quote the point Benveniste had made. Rather he wrote (in the passage in his essay on "Subjectivity in Language" that seems closest to whatever it was I remembered, or transformed in memory):

> Consciousness of self is only possible if it is experienced by contrast. I use *I* only when I am speaking to someone who will be a *you* in my address. It is this condition of dialogue that is constitutive of person, for it implies that reciprocally *I* becomes *you* in the address of the one who in his turn designates himself as *I*... If we seek a parallel to this we will not find it. The condition of man in language is unique.
>
> And so the old antinomies of "I" and "the other," of the individual and society, fail.

And again:

> [W]hat does *I* refer to? To something very peculiar which is exclusively linguistic: *I* refers to the act of individual discourse in which it is pronounced, and by this it designates the speaker. It is a term that cannot be identified except in what we have called elsewhere an instance of discourse and that has only

a momentary reference. The reality to which it refers
is the reality of the discourse.

Benveniste is telling us that solipsism is not merely a
moral failing, but a logical impossibility. Without you,
there is no I (not, as Benveniste also makes clear, the
same as "without me, there is no you.") And, now I
look further, I see that he did indeed make clear, stun-
ningly and yet quickly, as if in passing, the relation of
temporality to subjectivity as well: the "'present' ... has
only a linguistic fact as temporal reference: the coincidence of the event described with the instance of
discourse that describes it."

That "instant of discourse," as Benveniste has
already explained, entails in turn that unbalanced but
equal exchange whereby "I" becomes "you" and then
"you" becomes "I." So perhaps I remembered his point
correctly after all.

It's a humbling and terrifying one. It makes me
think, now, of a story by Harlan Ellison that I read
perhaps while still a teenager, titled "I Have No Mouth
and I Must Scream." Ellison wrote there in the voice of
the last sentient thing on earth, something that had no
way to express itself, no one to whom it might express
itself, and no way to kill itself either. Imagine the horror
of being eternally stuck in the position of "*I*." But that,
thankfully, would be inhuman, for we at least are mortal.

Second, I hoped (that word! It may come up
again) that in this renewed correspondence I might ask
Martin to try to explain, once again and in the language
of those who aren't physicists, what he meant by a
physical theory of dual temporalities, in which, for
example, there exist both a 1939 of 1939 and a 1939 of
2006, or perhaps more pertinently as we still dwell with

the prospect of a silent future, a 2039 of 2006 and a 2039 of 2039. (He tried to explain it once already, back in the 2004 of 2004, but I suppose I wasn't entirely "present.") If no one is there to hear it, will there still be a 2039 of 2039? And what does it mean to ask that question "now?"

Third, I proposed that we think more about the seemingly fatal linkage of critique, disaster, and futility, that is, about the old college saying that in the game of life, understanding is the booby prize. Why, if we aim to view even the prospect of extinction rationally, should we be captive to the spiraling sense that our lack of power is fueled not least by our own sense of powerlessness? We shouldn't; but we are.

And the last line Jonathan wrote on 7/20/2006 was:

>*Does this make any sense?*

Then,

On 7/21/06, Jonathan Boyarin wrote something like the following:

>*Here are my bits, for now:*

1) Films of Ralph Bakshi: I think a key cultural motif for both of us is the scene in Wizards *where the bad brother's two goons come for a couple of rabbis in long white caftans. They say, "Okay, but just give us a couple of minutes," at which point they start into this completely undignified vaudeville act in which they're trying to get God's attention. There's a bit of Yiddish thrown into it, notably the phrase* di gantse velt *(the whole world). They hit each other, they climb up and down ladders, and eventually one of the goons says, "Time's up" and shoots both of them.*

Why does it move us so?

Why is it all the more forceful because the word "Jew" is never mentioned?

What is the relation of this scene to the one near the end of the movie, where the "good" wizard, just before offing his Hitler brother with a pistol, says "I'm glad you changed your last name, you son of a bitch!"

How do we untangle the anti-Nazi message of that film from its Heideggerian anti-technological neo-Romanticism? Why would it even be a useful critical exercise to do so, rather than an amusing academic parlor game?

2) Benjamin quote: Unfortunately I don't have a copy of Illuminations *here in New York, but I can look this up easily enough when I get back to Kansas (or maybe you have the book); in the Introduction by Hannah Arendt (student of Heidegger, if we need a* smikhes haparshe *to my point 1) she quotes him as saying that if we don't resolve our species-wide historical predicament, "the planet will not forgive us." Again, if that was prescient, does prescience help us in any way, and if not, why does it even attract our interest?*

["Smikhes haparshe," another bit of Yiddish/Hebrew, refers to the rhetorical connection between a weekly portion of the Pentateuch read in the synagogue on the Sabbath, and the reading from the Prophets and Writings for that same Sabbath. It is already used ironically, by Yiddish writers such as Sholem-Aleykhem, to indicate the fragmentation of meaning in modernity. The quote from Benjamin in Arendt's introduction to *Illuminations* reads:

On this planet a great number of civilizations have perished in blood and horror. Naturally, one must wish for the planet that one day it will experience a civilization that has abandoned blood and horror; in fact, I am... inclined to assume that our planet is waiting for this. But it is terribly doubtful whether we can bring such a present to its hundred- or four-hundred-millionth birthday party. And if we don't, the planet will finally punish us, its unthoughtful well-wishers, by presenting us with that Last Judgment.

Well, maybe Benjamin was merely adding, as a postscript to the famous nineteenth-century Communist slogan, "...but most likely, barbarism."

And while I'm still writing in brackets, let me introduce the next item. You have no reason to know that I was pained, in previous correspondence, by Martin's quick and almost allergic reaction to my desire to discuss the continuing relevance of the messianic. (Or indeed that Martin lives in Jerusalem, where the messianic and the annihilationist are often indistinguishable.) And I should also tell you that "Heschel's portrait of the Kotsker" refers to a book written in Yiddish by Abraham Joshua Heschel, about a Hasidic master who waged an implacable and ultimately fatal war against self-deception.]

3) *Status of the messianic: You and I have not resolved our communication on this big theme. I continue to have the sense that you cut off the possibility of a more generous reading of this impulse because of the destructive irrationalism with which it is almost exclusively associated in Israel, elsewhere in the Jewish world and in the Christian world today. (Indeed, one of the large themes that "time and language*

now" might encompass is the collapse of, and distinctions between, the affect of themes such as the messianic now and in the past.) You phrase the impulse only as a (wrong-headed) alternative to facing the abyss. That may well be an appropriate characterization of some earlier messianisms, and it promises to give me some grasp on how I relate, today, to Heschel's portrait of the Kotsker, something I will have to do in the coming months.

Obviously, this is a theme that was vitally important for me, as a younger person, in conceiving a vital linkage between my desire for transgenerational Jewish identification and my desire for human redemption. I think it would be useful to work together at trying to articulate the relations between messianism as an impulse to do more than just muddle through and messianism as an alternative to the abyss, especially since it appears more and more that "muddling through" isn't much of an option. We have been too successful not to suffer terribly from our imperfections; "the planet will not forgive us."

4) Minnesota: When I gave my lecture on "Extinction and Difference" at the University of Minnesota, one of the junior members of the anthropology department, a physical anthropologist, told me how much it meant to him that I had acknowledged the real contingency of human culture. As he told me, one of the things he tries to impress upon his students is that our inheritance of language is not a given. "If it stopped for a generation, the whole thing would be lost." (Speaking of "inheritance" suggests that Derrida's Specters of Marx *might be pertinent for this project as well. Do you need a copy?)*

5) Personal ambition: I catch myself in the course of writing these notes thinking, "Oooh, ooh, ooh, people are going to be really impressed when they read this!" And then I feel embarrassed. And then I remember Heschel's warning that "Anyone who spends an hour in the Kotsker's presence will never taste self-satisfaction again."

[Solipsism is worse than death.
    What will Martin write?
    Man, I gotta get something to eat.]

thln_002 (Martin)

Before getting into the content, there are some mechanical issues that come to mind. First, I am writing this paragraph on the assumption that at some future time we will prefer to have kept the entire record of our exchange in one text format (as opposed to "principle content" in Word, delivered with meta-text in an email cover letter). That's why I'm making these comments in the Word file—they can be edited out later, but experience has shown that over time it gets more and more difficult to distinguish content from meta-content, while maintaining the discipline to insure that everything gets filed in the right place. Second, some system of numbering and cross referencing the contributions will be necessary. I called this file THLN_002 (*Time and Human Language Now*—part 2) and it'll probably be sufficient for Jonathan to send odd-numbered files and Martin to send even numbered files (the leading 00 will help the computer's file system keep them in order, taking account the far fetched possibility that the number of separate files may reach 100). It may also eventually become necessary to number paragraphs, but I'm not getting that crazy yet.

As you have probably discerned from Jonathan's opening, this book, a record of our dialogue on human language, touches on many apparently disparate themes, but is acutely concerned with the desire for redemption. Jonathan alludes to several themes we might normally associate with redemption— organized prayer, especially prayers of mourning, collective delivery from political/historical catastrophe, millennial collapse of civilization, messianic salvation— and to more personal redemptions—escape from isolation and achievement of personal ambition. But ultimately he asks us to recognize the redemptive character of ordinary human language, and expresses the hope that we can leverage this recognition into an effective will to forestall our own extinction. His intent, as I understand it, is not just to recommend "talking it over" as a solution to the dangers facing the world, even though an apparent decline in preference (even the fashionably disingenuous kind) for discussion instead of violence is among the greatest of those dangers. Rather, in the elementary act of speaking, he identifies the germ of an intellectually sound counterargument to the dominant nihilism of neo liberalism, and hopes that thinking about language can improve the prospects that we will have a future of any kind. What follows is our attempt to elaborate this argument, itself evolving as an ongoing example of our topic.

Describing the origins of this project, Jonathan tells us that during a brief exchange of words, drawing on a mix of English, Hebrew, and Yiddish (to which he now adds ancient Greek, by translating the old fashioned word *shul* as the older *synagogue*), he suddenly found himself astonished at the very possibility of mundane communication by language. In part, that astonishment expresses a basic tension underlying many disciplines, linguistics among them, between the utterly commonplace phenomena they study and the notorious difficulty of giving a scholarly account of those phenomena and their origins. Physicists considering ordinary gravity as the geometry of a four-dimensional space time, possibly imbedded in a series of higher dimensional universes, occasionally experience a similar bewilderment. I recently confronted another form of this tension while preparing a lecture on information theory for undergraduates in computer science. Computation-based communication technologies are often designed to mimic the externally observable features of human language, and these algorithms can be reasonably well understood, even when the details of the original human "implementation" are only vaguely known. After I remarked on the seemingly "miraculous" quality of human communication, Janet (the wise woman in my life) quipped, "Only a man would call it a miracle that people communicate. Women communicate all the time." Having thus gendered the discourse, I admitted that invoking the category of the miraculous implied no appeal to supernatural explanation, but was an expression of spontaneous awe at how much about communication is not currently (or perhaps, in principle) amenable to scientific analysis, despite the heavy reliance on communication in the scientific method. Science loves fables of sudden insight such as Jonathan's—Archimedes running naked from his bath shouting "eureka" or Isaac Newton hit on the head by a falling apple—because the first revelations of deep scientific truth are generally found in seemingly trivial, yet empirically undeniable, observations about the small and the local, those commonplace shared experiences that are precisely the field of applicability of the scientific method. Like Archimedes's buoyancy and

Newton's gravity, language represents a profound dynamical universe, and for all the difficulty in explaining those dynamics, science (like women?) accepts language and communication as mundane, observable fact, readily taken for granted, and empirically indisputable. Therefore, the logical inferences drawn from language by linguistics, psychology, and other disciplines, rest on a firm foundation (a response to those who would dispute the existence of language from outside the context of language is beyond the scope of this work), and are themselves a reliable basis for technological application in fields from speech therapy to computer architecture. In plain language, the implications of verbal communication regarding the nature of human beings and their relationships cannot be dismissed as "junk science" or "only" a theory. To take seriously the intersubjectivity of speaker and listener is not an academic parlor game to be safely ignored by determined men with "other priorities." When we ignore Benveniste's insights into the personal pronouns, we consequently think and plan poorly, and we ignore at our own peril (for example) Jessica Benjamin's observations about the traumatic effect of being left to feel unrecognized. The cozy habits of hegemony that deny the unbalanced symmetry inherent in relationship, and deprive the other of any standing from which to appropriate the word I and address authority as you, are the "quaint" and "obsolete" notions, in an age when the risk of epidemic and climatic disaster makes no exceptions for the powerful, and threats of overwhelming military force do not intimidate, but are met with an almost joyful willingness to depart this world in a last desperate attainment of parity in death. The basic logical inferences that derive from the nature of human communication provide us with more than a romantic sense of awe about what it means to be human—they also provide guidelines for how we must behave if we wish to survive.

Unlike previous world crises such as the nuclear arms race, the greatest dangers we face today are not the potential consequences of a fatal act, but the potentially fatal consequences of failing to act. Following 50 years of cold war, we have developed a certain limited confidence that nuclear confrontation will not inevitably lead to annihilation, because it is—or at least was—widely understood that mutual destruction is assured once certain steps have been taken. But now, we require an act of coordinated, communicated, and collective action, changing the behavior of individuals and institutions in order to prevent a calamity that still seems remote and implausible to most people. The tense narrative of nuclear escalation created a vocabulary of noir images that effectively prompted millions to compel world leaders to step back from the button and keep their hands in plain sight. But for the time being, global plague and environmental collapse are seen as diffuse abstractions, and it seems unlikely that we are capable of organizing ourselves—and willing to make sacrifices in advance—to rescue ourselves from risks so far outside our experience. As in the arms race, communication by symbols of likely devastation, such as Gore's image of Florida under water or Lovelock's image of a Martian desert landscape here on earth may help make the issues more concrete, if they are not too frightening. But the range and scope of changes—not disarming missiles, but changing the consumption habits of the entire developed world—and the level of coordination necessary to manage that change will require a new appreciation of human language and communication. Communicating only through the language of the marketplace will not enable humanity to survive the next few decades. In the age of global corporations, global climate change, and a global war on terror, the very notion that human needs can be addressed by individuals or even nations attending to their private, local concerns seems like a prescription for busy work. If the long-term goal is, at very least, survival, then we will have to take advantage of the human facility for communication, and the more nuanced forms of negotiation and accommodation implicit in language, and do so in the global context. This kind of redemption is ultimately a precondition for the others.

I was not initially motivated to begin this project in order to argue that disastrous climate change can be avoided. My initial thinking was a more mundane exchange of insights and experiences, between an anthropologist and a physicist, who have looked at human communication from different corners of the world-laboratory. I assumed from the start that the different perspectives would be interesting to members of related fields, as well as to readers with no connection to either discipline. Jonathan's suggestion also provides an opportunity to pursue a long standing interest in examining the different ways that language is used in contemporary science and the humanities. Even at this early stage, the diversity of our associations to the topic surprises me, and my current feeling is that the project itself—producing this interaction as an evolving discourse between active researchers in different academic fields—is more interesting than the particular expertise that either of us brings to the subject. Because this little book is an actual record of dialog (an oddball example of the dialectical method known in Hebrew as "chevrusa"), not a narrative device created in one mind,

I expect to continue to be surprised, challenged, and hope that something useful emerges in the end.

Jonathan—I want to send this to you, because it has been too long in hatching. I did get a good running start in defining my own approach to this project, and that has gotten me very excited about it (I'm having trouble not sounding like a record producer). Still, there are important parts of your opening that I haven't even begun to address in writing, and I haven't written my reactions to Benveniste's article or how it seems to fit in with other bits of contemporary thinking. Many of the ideas are in my head, but I want you to see where my thinking is heading while I write.

In terms of the beginnings of a table of contents, I agree with the suggestions you made:

- Benveniste—his paper is interesting to me, both for what he argues, which is central to what we're trying to do, and for the "traditional philosophical" approach he takes, defining terms and then making and backing-up claims. He's not trying to sweep us along, he's trying to show that if you take him seriously, then you have to accept his conclusions. There is a huge amount of material here. Obviously, it also connects with the idea of the intersubjective, and all sorts of other critical theory stuff.

- Time—I would love to give a non-technical explanation in more detail. This also connects to Benveniste, who argues that "now" means the time I mark-off by speaking about "now."

    Now this "present" in its turn has only a linguistic fact as temporal reference: the coincidence of the event described with the instance of discourse that describes it. The temporal referent of the present can only be internal to the discourse.

I used a similar idea in a paper a few years ago, asking the question, "To the extent that time is subjective, how do two particles 'know' how to coordinate their times, that is, agree on what they call 'now'?" The answer I gave turned out to be similar to Benveniste's and the results were fundamental to the problem of relating the "two-time" picture to the usual "one-time" picture.

- Understanding cannot be the booby prize, because if we do not take seriously in the global arena the consequences of what language says about who and what we are, we can easily follow our noses into disaster (in the sense of "prisoners' dilemma" and any number of other game theory results). In physics, there are many areas in which the global behavior (over long times and large distances) of a system can be very different from the small incremental changes that determine the global behavior. This is the basis of complexity. Changes in weather systems can be predicted accurately on the basis of theory over small areas and short times (a few days), but the equations cannot be solved exactly and approximations are subject to the "butterfly effect"—small changes in initial conditions lead to enormous changes over a relatively short time. Understanding is only the booby prize if we agree to see ourselves as lemmings. The neo-liberals may never understand what hits them, but they cannot win this time, and if they are allowed to make the decisions, then it's "game over." The Midrash you raise on this topic, from Ralph Bakshi to Walter Benjamin, are all relevant, and we can find much more.

- Meshiach—I'm not sure that we're as far apart as you think. I do not deny the possibility of messianic rescue. I just think that HaKaBa ("G-d") posed the brit (the deal with the Israelites) on the ground rules that we'll try to hold up our end as if no supernatural bailout is possible (and if it is, then it's none of our business). While this interpretation does put a barrier in the path of the destructive irrationalism you mention (because it disqualifies the impulse to violate the brit and, then "Jew Him down" on the price of salvation, as an anti-Semitic stereotype), it is not designed to do that. It has more to do with a general outlook about our place in the world—if one single act of human-initiated magic is admissible into the discourse of what we may reliably count on in this life, then there is simply no point whatsoever of trying to escape solipsism. If miracles occur as empirical events, then we have to take note of them and observe our in-principle inability to explain them. And if we want to incorporate miracles into the "technology" of daily life, and propose an efficacy of prayer (or even acts) that includes the possibility of even semi-reliably generating miracles upon demand, then I don't really see much point in preferring rationalism to irrationalism. I'm not sure that is fair to the messianist viewpoint, but I am comfortable leaving it this way: if future miracles occur, then we will find out about them when they do. To be continued…

- Other possible topics include:
  - The relationship of Benveniste's view of what we do when we speak to Chomsky's view of what we do when we listen, and how these two must obviously be integrated in us somehow
  - The relation of all this to computer language and computer communication
  - Kristeva's idea about hospitality (*a'halan wa sa'halan*) being the fundamentally human act, and how "my" willingness to allow "you" to refer to yourself as "I" can be a form of hospitality

- Looking at other conclusions from linguistics that might inform a post marketplace view of human relations
- The near-simultaneous emergence of scientific claims of imminent climatic catastrophe, apocalyptic millenarianism among fundamentalist Jews and Christians, and suicide terrorism—is Death the new Life?

• We should be open to other ideas that come up as we do this.

thln_003 (Jonathan)

Here are two mistakes I've made, one about e-mail in particular and one about the internet:

First, some years ago (as early as the late 1980s, I think) when, through our friend Ari Davidow who moderated the first "Jewish discussion group" on the WELL, one of the first "electronic bulletin boards," I first became acquainted with both e-mail and online discussion groups, I was briefly excited at the possibility that here was a genuinely new medium for participatory democracy. It struck me that one of the major problems with existing democratic structures is that they are rarely designed so that important decisions are made by that set of people whom they affect (as opposed, for example, to those formally authorized to take part in whatever deliberative decision-making occurs at the level of a state, with regard to whatever matters have historically come within the purview of that state). It wouldn't, I thought, have meant that everyone would have to be involved in every decision, but rather that flexible enough discussion groups could be created so that decisions (let's say, with respect to sustainable ocean harvests) could be made by "bodies" of electronic correspondents with an interest in the outcome of those sets of decisions. Why I would denigrate this now as an out-and-out "mistake" is, first, that the vision assumes a collective rather than selfish interest on the part of every (or at least a sufficient plurality) of participants, and that it assumes a distribution of power, that is of the means of coercion, commensurate with the distribution of the means of articulation. But perhaps here is a germ of a vision (of course I don't suppose I'm the only one who's had it) to respond to your challenge that we think differently than "the cozy habits of hegemony that deny the unbalanced symmetry inherent in relationship."

Second, at a time I can no longer specify, at the Center for Studies of Social Change at the New School, in response to a question after some guest lecture I gave, I denied that the internet was a place of significant formation of personal identities. Perhaps I was thinking of the pseudonymous "tags" of some internet correspondents, and thinking of them as merely epiphenomenal; more likely, I suppose, I was intent on defending face-to-face encounters as the place where "true" identities are created and sustained.

That I would not give the same answer now is not only a result of the extraordinary efflorescence of electronic communication, nor only of the abandonment of any supposition that it is in physical contiguity and in aural meeting that "true" identity is created. The hunch here was that there is a certain affinity between "presence" in space (being, here) and "the present" in time (being, now) such that interpersonal identity—

being, fully, a person—would require both simultaneity and proximity. But that co-presence and simultaneity are the only true grounds of interpersonal identity are undermined, for "me personally," by repeated retrievals (through simple internet searches) of figures from the past (a beloved teacher, a beloved friend) and the experience of creating with them, sight unseen after decades, a new "present" through this medium. E-mail, as clunky and near-obsolete to those of our children's generation as snail-mail letters now seem to you and me: but still, a possibility of recuperating lost fragments of "my" identity at which I am still capable of being amazed.

Edmond Jabès asserts: "You are silent, I was; you speak, I am." I had always thought of this in terms of the possibility of a living relationship with the dead. (In anthropological terms, there is nothing magical or superstitious about such a possibility; it would be, rather, almost a truism in nearly all human lifeworlds save the post-Enlightenment. If language, symbol-making, culture, created as they arose the problem of acute consciousness of individual mortality, their evolution was in turn also driven as the solution to that problem.) Taken as a statement about the politics of memory, this would be consonant with Benjamin's injunction to us to rescue our dead from that enemy "who has not ceased to be victorious." I had always thought, that is, of Jabès' "I" here in the guise of one dead, of Jabès in fact as a speaker for the dead. Speaking of the dead, then, in a way that rescues them "from a conformity that is about to overpower them" would be a way of preserving life, would address and limit in some way the death of the dead. In this attempt to translate between Jabès' injunction and

Benjamin's, pastness (having been, "I was") would be analogous to death, as presence (being, "I am") would be analogous to life.

But in the light of Benveniste's discussion of presence and the second person, now I think of reading Jabès differently, not as a deceased petitioner for recognition, but as a co-present interlocutor, as someone sitting in a room with his fellow. What he would then be saying is that "I" comes into being, is, in the act of listening and not (or not necessarily so much) in the act of speaking. We are used to thinking of humanity as "the speaking animal;" does our survival require that we learn to become listening animals? In any case, "you are silent, I was" is a logically puzzling statement. I have to resist not listening to it, have to resist shouting back at it (another way of not listening to it), have to resist, also, sullen silence in response to it; unless (taking the statement seriously) I am willing to risk my fellow's not being, or more precisely his having been (reading "was" here as equivalent to "have been"). What is the ontology of "having been?" Is it possible for all speakers only "to have been," if there is no one to speak and thus to make them "be" (again)? And one (even God!) wouldn't be enough for us to have been, I suppose, since (in Jabès' formulation) one must speak for another to be. If there is no pair of speakers at last (no last couple, staring backward at Adam and Eve) will it be as though all of us, even the renowned among us, "had never been," *kilo hayu*, as the morning prayer has it?

How can we compare, in turn, the inflection of "having been" to any possible inflection of "will be?" Let's suppose (I suppose even that this is true, in the sense that archives would bear the supposition out, but I think it doesn't matter whether such truth obtains) that throughout the early 1940s, the lights of Broadway never dimmed while the gas chambers of Europe were in full operation. What does it mean to suppose, to state that, "now?" Keep in mind that confessional rhetoric such as this, about the failure of someone or some collective to recognize a threat that was contemporaneous to some past time (1943 on Broadway, 1943 at Auschwitz) is not only a judgment passed on a certain "having been," but also always an implicit statement about what someone or some collective should be doing, differently, in the present. How, conversely, should we speak for example of Billy Joel's song "Miami 2017 (The Night the Lights Went Out on Broadway)," which would have been I guess in the late nineteen-seventies—a future imagined in our past that has never happened... yet?

In any case public discourse, here synagogue prayer, skirts away rapidly from the articulation of a possible never having been. You say that God sent us out into time without a safety net. Perhaps. But this very prayer of human (and of Jewish, Israelite) self-abnegation is followed with a hasty assertion: "But we are Your people, members of Your covenant," a reassurance of some kind of collective eternity. Does God continue speaking, then? It would be more than presumptuous to say yes or no. What we might say, instead, is that this nation, this collective, this *anakhnu*, does not "exist" except in its relation to You. God is that partner—but wait, I am not a theologian, not in the business of saying what God "is" (maybe God also "is" only when we speak.) Rather, maybe our survival will be enhanced by thinking of God as the partner who makes it possible for us to continue to be so long as we are listeners.

If being is always and only a matter of presence constituted as an effect of dialogue, there "is" no future; no future to speak of, anyhow, and even if it is much easier, somehow, to think of a past or pasts as existing through dialogue with the dead. Is it any comfort to think that in any case there "is" no future? Jabès says this as well, that "We are all without future—I responded—Tomorrow is nothing but the hope, naively maintained, of better days to come." But why would we think that, when we have so many *feared* futures? That all of our futures may be "imaginary" makes them no less consequential, it only reminds us that the consequences are not necessarily a "coming to be" of that which we imagine, hope, or fear.

"You are silent, I was; you speak, I am" is, if suggestive, still terribly, awesomely stark, with no clue as to how the dialogue is to be formed, how "you" and "I" are to trade places so that, let's say, "I" retain some identity even as "I" speak. Perhaps the suggestion is that my only true response constitutes a continuing-to-listen to you, so that you too are still speaking, allowing me to "be" even I speak in turn? I can only be stimulated, and not bound, by your "Table of Contents" in a book of dialogue that waits to be written (the wise French convention is to place the table of contents at the end of the book.) How then shall I respond to your "bullet points" (a jarring idiom of violent death, here, but are we trying to keep some cruel world at bay or rather to listen inside the whirlwind?) Some speak to references I already have so that I am able to fill them out, as a reader, even before filling them out in writing, as a respondent; others remain semilegible to me, as no doubt to other readers, because you and I do not of course share a full but only a partial (and rich!) set of referents.

One of your references that I already have, then: "understanding is not the booby prize." What *I* know is that you are here addressing our younger selves, as we first knew each other; you are rethinking, if not refuting, something that we, good college Marxists, believed. We meant to distance ourselves from an ethic of detached or "idealistic" contemplation, from the notion that the search for comprehension is the greatest goal of life. Supposing that the philosophers had "only" interpreted the world, in various ways, but the point is to change it—we failed to acknowledge what I think we nevertheless already also understood, which is that interpretation is also a work in the world. A young Marx asserted also that "man [sic] makes himself." That we have used language largely at least to unmake ourselves does not mean Marx was wrong, it just means that self-making was always a dangerous game.

And a question sparked by another of your references that I have, but more vague, etched on my mind not with the acid of nostalgia for our passionate and cynical youth but in the fading vigor of some passing e-mail of yours, the mention of the name of Julia Kristeva, a lecture she gave (am I right so far?) that you heard in Jerusalem, something you told me about that lecture that led me to associate the title *[The Book] of Hospitality* not with its author's name, Jacques Derrida, but with hers; a thought in any case of the continuing *mitzvah* of hospitality, taken together (in one thought, as a challenge to imagine simultaneously problems that seem to be situated on vastly incommensurate scales) with your call for "an act of coordinated, communicated, and collective action" at the level of the species (*at the level of the species!*) and with Bill McKibben's reminder that part of the difficulty we have in recognizing, let alone acting together, to address the current crisis is that it has largely been produced as a side effect of technologies "freeing" us to be further apart, less connected, less in communication with one another: How to restore face-to-face I and you without sacrificing common human consciousness? (Lest such "consciousness" might seem merely "moral," remember that if understanding is a matter of survival and not just the booby prize, ethics, too, is a matter of life and death.)

Our concept of the interpersonal, of the face-to-face, is closely tied with our notion of the local, and it is easy to resort to a notion that the solution to our crisis lies in a reduced vision of human settlement on earth, such as a limited set of villages in appropriate environments (those that do not require massive amounts of excess carbon transfer), with such communications and other exchange between them as is necessary and appropriate to a more or less steady environmental state. But what exclusions—"racial," geographical, sexual—lie buried in any conceivable journey from now to there? Take, for illustration, a project that I consider to be eminently worthwhile, that of *localizing* the effects of massive "climate change" (oddly neutral term!) and its attendant social effects (e.g., what might Lawrence, Kansas be like as a bio-environment 15, 20, 50 years from now)? If there is any human value in "planning" at all, this is surely a project that should be well underway by now. But we are talking, really, about the "downsizing" of the species, and the only thing we really know how to plan for (if that) is growth. What are the implications, especially ethical, of engaging in such an enterprise of projected shrinkage, a retreat to the regional? Are we prepared to surrender a species-wide conversation and say that only some of us need participate? And what is the source of a persisting arrogance that assumes that, because it is possible (thanks to the Internet) for you and I to have this dialogue "now," a larger one we might project would presumably include us? What I mean is: just because we project concern about the ethics of being in a privileged position does not guarantee that we will turn out in the end to have been privileged.

A suggestion: "the local," even "place," is not as fixed as our maps suggest, but is a contingent effect of language or, if that sounds like a postmodern platitude, more sharply that language is "place." One thing we can almost be certain of about the future is that we are not moving toward the kind of localism envisaged by the "village model" of which I have just written, if only because there is so much contingency and so little we know that the future will not be anything that we imagine now. But perhaps thinking carefully about the taking-place of our speaking may help get us into the habit of remembering the boundaries, the inclusions and exclusions of the sphere of mutual responsibility, the human places that we are always creating and destroying through language.

Tell me more, perhaps, about Kristeva?

thln_004 (Martin)

Julia Kristeva is here, but that will have to wait a bit to be articulated. By your act of hospitality—by making room for my words at your table—you accept the obligation to hear my narrative, but also to suffer my narrative style, which will be difficult to follow unless I first explain my use of certain ideas from theoretical physics, especially time, space, interaction, and prediction. Although my original intention was to quickly introduce a few abstract terms for later use, this digression has ballooned into several pages of occasionally dense discourse, and while the conclusions are relevant to our broader topic, the discussion itself may appear as something of a long detour. The divergence between intent and outcome can be attributed to a teacher's narcissistic impulse to explain, or (equivalently?) to an irresistible anxiety that these conclusions, taken out of context and without simple examples, will give the impression of magic or superstition. As an aid in reading the full discussion, or perhaps as an alternative, I will first summarize my main conclusions. The purpose of the following section is to establish how contemporary physics grounds itself in these claims:

> 1. Physics builds models from three ingredients: idealized entities, relationships that characterize interaction among these entities, and physical principles that connect seemingly independent changes in these relationships over time. When the analog of an empirical phenomenon can be recognized in a model, the model is said to explain the phenomenon, despite numerous problems of interpretation that belong to philosophy of science.

2.   Spatial and temporal distances are largely equivalent forms of separation. The quantitative expression of physical interactions often depends on the physical configuration, that is, on how objects are separated in space-time.

3.   The notion of space and time as an empty arena of infinite extent is a convenient but arbitrary and potentially confusing picture. Physical theories must be conceptually independent of this picture, and not depend on how any observer defines a frame of reference by assigning coordinates in that arena.

4.   In his younger years, Einstein conceived of the past, present, and future coexisting in different parts of an unchanging four-dimensional space-time. In this picture, for as-yet unexplained reasons, individual consciousness can look into three spatial directions, but experiences time as moving from point to point with no depth perception in the time direction. But this "block universe," besides posing mathematical and conceptual problems for modern physics, allows for no real change, other than the inexorable motion of human consciousness through the predetermined script written into our trajectory through space-time. In order to re-introduce dynamical evolution to physics, an additional measure of time must be defined.

5.   Spatial and temporal separations characterize the physical configuration at a given chronological moment. This moment is determined by the flow of historical time, identical for all observers, and always moving forward. The change in space-time configuration from one historical moment to another is called evolution, and represents the physical influence of relationship on the interacting objects, not merely shifting points of view between frames of

reference. The four space-time separations are dynamical variables—they evolve as the historical time advances, in turn affecting the quantitative form of the interaction through its dependence on the system configuration.

6. The causal principle is that events at one historical time cannot affect events at an earlier historical time. Nevertheless, temporal separation, known as coordinate time or Einstein time and measured on conventional clocks, can change direction as the historical time advances, so that events observed as temporally sequential according to a laboratory clock may have actually occurred in a very different historical order. Therefore, physical models provide different kinds of "predictions" about the future—a prediction of how the physical configuration will evolve as the historical time evolves, and another prediction of how the physical configuration at a particular historical time will appear in a laboratory at some past or future temporal separation. So, the correct statement of how some deterministic physical system will look in 25 years may change significantly over historical time. Similarly, it may be possible to "travel backward in time" (appear at values of the clock/calendar that we currently regard as the past), but it is not clear what we will observe and what kind of interactions we will be able to experience. We will certainly not be able to change events that occurred at earlier historical times.

7. A physical explanation of observed phenomena requires that we understand how the relationships among the participants induce evolution over chronological times, how those relationships depend on the spatial and temporal separation of the participants, and how the relationships themselves may evolve as chronological time advances.

Metaphorically, this summary can be seen as an example of how the modern view of time can be applied—in the reader's frame of reference the summary appears before the full discussion, despite having evolved in the opposite historical order. Having said all that, I hope that my earlier suggestion of a tentative table of contents appears less demanding in this context—it was nothing more than a prediction of a possible future at one unprivileged moment of history. The projected contents may be an entirely correct forecast of the future as of today and yet be replaced tomorrow—if that were not the case, then we would be constrained to merely follow the plan set for us in pre-ancient times, and our understanding would indeed be a frustrating booby prize.

As I noted earlier, despite any institutional barriers scientists may erect in practice, the starting point of empirical science—taken as a philosophical method, not itself the object of empirical anthropology, and side-stepping any argument about whether that separation is possible—is the act of observing ordinary events, something we share in an inherently democratic and egalitarian manner. Nevertheless, the success of Newtonian physics, and the authority awarded its method by Enlightenment thinkers, continues to exert undue influence on our view of reality and our use of language, imposing unnecessary restrictions on what we consider to be a reasonable interpretation of everyday experience. In particular, the mathematical entities called space and time, as defined by classical physicists who found these definitions useful, have in many cases replaced our wider intuitive understandings of place and temporality. Ironically, when we presume that common experiences like "internal clock" or "personal space" must be explained by reduction to the "real" time read on clocks and the "objective" space measured with rulers, we are not only confusing our actual experience with tropes for a particular analytical methodology, we are also ignoring that physics itself has evolved beyond mechanistic Enlightenment determinism. If insights from theoretical physics are going to be useful as evocative symbols in non-technical discourse, it is necessary to bring their conventional usage into the twenty-first century, at the same time avoiding the opposite misconception—that contemporary physics has adopted a postmodern relativism that can say almost nothing certain about a random universe. So, without claiming that physics can make any specific scientific contribution to understanding our internal time sense, it can offer a more nuanced vocabulary for discussing the associated sensations. I emphasize that these contemporary formulations—despite sounding like something lifted from a magical pre-Enlightenment lifeworld—are the insights that science has found useful in describing the universe as a theatre of physical relationships. And despite the obvious fact that it is precisely the power of scientific insight that necessitates the discussion of manmade climate change, I make no other claim for the value of these notions, other than as a useful vocabulary for thinking about the issues you raise.

The general method of theoretical physics, adopted from its antecedents in ancient mathematics and philosophy, is to first posit simple objects—rarified abstractions exhibiting a limited number of characteristics—that exist in a specified relationship to one another, and then extract from these idealized models, analogs to the behavior we observe in real life. So, classical mechanics posits a type of object called a point mass (an object with measurable mass, but no size or any other physical characteristic), a set of specific relationships between objects (especially gravitational attraction and springiness), and a set of mathematical rules (calculus and Newton's laws) that express how changes over time in one aspect of a relationship correlate with changes in another aspect. Assembling these abstract elements in various ways, Newton's laws describe analogs of a huge number of observable phenomena, and in the jargon of physics one says that a model "explains" a phenomenon, meaning that one can describe a highly reduced microcosm in which an analog of the phenomenon can be identified. At the scale of the solar system, the particular relationship called gravitation "explains" the observed motions of the planets, while at a more human scale, this same relationship "explains" apples falling from trees (but also predicts the trajectory of a cannonball) at great accuracy. While the notion of a point mass, lacking size, color, flavor, chemical composition, ontogeny, teleology, and all the rest, is clearly a wild abstraction from human experience, the notion of a specified relationship is no less intangible. This kind of relationship is often, but not necessarily, described as a force between the related objects, directed from one point mass to the other, or more generally as a physical interaction that unites the interacting objects as partners. The interaction may change its form, strength and direction of influence "dynamically" (progressively over time), but we nevertheless identify the essential qualitative relationship as unchanged, because the quantitative changes in the outward expression of the interaction can be consistently associated with corresponding changes in the separation of the interacting parties. For example, the gravitational interaction between two point masses weakens when the distance between masses increases, while the spring interaction grows stronger when the distance increases. The separation of the point masses is then considered a dynamical variable, a feature of the physical circumstances that affects the quantitative form of the relationship, but cannot change its essential qualitative nature. So, as we stretch a rubber band around one hand, waiting for our next sentence to miraculously appear on the page, we think of the changing force around our fingers as a specified abstract interaction reacting quantitatively to our play, not as a sequence of separate relationships with different origin myths and significances. For all the arguable success of this abstract approach in "explaining" the motions of planets, cannonballs and rubber bands, claims that this deterministic thinking can be applied to human behavior are heard more from social scientists than from physicists.

Because the manifestation of a physical interaction usually depends on the geometrical configuration of the relevant objects, classical physicists found great utility in adopting Descartes' method of coordinates. Cartesian coordinates, familiar from high school algebra as the horizontal and vertical axes (usually called x and y) on which we draw graphs, can be extended to a three-dimensional grid, on which the location of a physical object is described as the height, width, and depth of some "point", as measured from some arbitrarily defined "origin". In simple terms, one is now doing high school geometry on graph paper, first specifying objects by the coordinates of their endpoints, and then describing shapes by calculating the lengths of the line segments that connect the endpoints. Similarly, it is possible to reformulate the mathematical description of physical interactions, replacing all references to physical distance with references to the coordinates (location) of the participating objects. Now as we play with the rubber band, we specify the five sets of coordinates describing the independent locations of our fingertips, and calculate the distances over which we are stretching the rubber, using the Pythagorean theorem and similar mathematical relationships. Although this approach has been a strategic success for physics, it subtly changes the underlying conception of the physical process in two significant ways. First, by emphasizing the individual location of each object, the coordinate method encourages us to regard systems as consisting of ontologically independent entities that enter interaction at some fortuitous moment only after they are wholly formed, rather than parts of a whole that owe their existence to the relationships that character- ize their species. For example, while ancient geometers viewed a triangle as an object with an intrinsic shape, algebraists describe it as three independent vertices determined by three sets of coordinates, and so draw- ing line segments between the vertices and making the shape of the triangle visible becomes a secondary matter. So, while Euclid's characterization of triangles by angles and lengths (distances) encourages the study of similarity between triangles, the algebraic approach makes it mathematically convenient to study how the shape of a triangle changes when just one of the vertices (coordinates) is shifted by some internal or external process. In this spirit, to explain a ball falling from our hand we are probably more inclined to invoke a "force of gravity" acting on the coordinates of the ball and pulling it to earth, rather than describe the earth and the ball as sharing a gravitational relationship that tends to minimize their separation by accelerating both objects. The development of physics in the past gener- ation has reemphasized the inherent unity of the massive particles and the relationships through which they come into existence, and much effort has been put into methods of solving problems that avoid regarding them as approximately independent. The second subtle change is that while conceptions of distance arise from our physical experience, Descartes' coordinate scheme formally describes an empty arena of infinite space through which physical bodies move and interactions occur. This notion of an empty physical space of infinite extent, presumably existing "out there" so as to endow the coordinate abstraction with an independent reality, was given a famously unfavorable reception when it was first introduced in the late renaissance, and by the mid-20th century, physics accepted that however useful it might be, it does not describe the shape of the universe. Standard gravitational theory and cosmology describe our universe as a curved space, covering unimaginably large separations in space and time, but not constituting an infinite empty arena, while more speculative theories conceive of space and time as emergent phenomena, thrown off as the consequence of more elementary processes.

Sorting out the coordinate method from the physical system begins with recalling that the coordinate axes are constructed arbitrarily as an abstract framework for "locating" the individual point masses, and that these individual "locations" only have meaning in relation to the arbitrarily chosen framework. An observer working from one perspective (choice of axes) will assign different coordinates to a given mass point than those measured by another observer viewing them from a different perspective (choice of axes), but using the Pythagorean theorem both will calculate the same distances between point masses. Therefore, unless we want to ascribe some deeper reality to the coordinate method, physical interactions should only depend on the relative separation of point masses, and be independent of how the arbitrary coordinate axes are drawn. Combining the requirement that fundamental physical interactions be independent of the choice of axes, with the Newtonian concept of a universal measure of time, flowing identically for all observers and unaffected by other physical conditions, one arrives at the principle of Galilean relativity. Einstein was led to reformulate the principle of relativity, demonstrating that the electromagnetic interactions and the well-known properties of light require that time be regarded as just another form of separation, equivalent in some sense to distance and measured as a coordinate along some arbitrary axis. Einstein's relativity principle requires that the fundamental interactions of physics be independent of the choice of the four axes of space-time—the three spatial directions and one time direction—known as the observer's frame of reference. Consequently, the measured passage of time is affected in part by the perspective of the observer, as is the observed simultaneity of separate events. In physics, the equivalence of space and time as forms of separation is limited by rules of causality that are required to make the distinction between present and future meaningful. However, in general language, these causal restrictions can be ignored, at least until we decide to ask what is not merely possible, but actual.

Einstein tended to view four-dimensional space-time as a "block universe"—a single unchanging four-dimensional structure, through which our consciousness moves for reasons we do not yet understand. In this view, the present simply denotes all space-time points with the same value of time as the locus of our consciousness, the past is all space-time points with an earlier value of time, and the future is all space-time points with a later value of time. In the block universe, it is our consciousness that is located at a particular value of time, but those sections of space-time known as the future and the past coexist with the present, separated by a temporal distance in the same way that a foreign country is separated by a spatial distance. This fixed universe must then either extend infinitely into the future, or lead to some moment at which time ends.

If time and space are truly equivalent, then it should be possible to find physical situations in which spatial and temporal separation are exchanged with respect to their usual interpretations. In analogy to a ball falling from our hand at some height above the ground, we may ask, in principle at least, whether we can swap spatial and temporal separation, and imagine an interaction that permits an object to be "lifted" into the future, so that when released it "falls" back into the present. There is some debate among physicists about this specific question, but ironically, a seemingly more farfetched experiment is routinely repeated millions of times every day in laboratories around the world, and so has effectively been verified to the same empirical degree as high school Euclidean geometry (a point emphasized by E. F. Taylor and J. A. Wheeler). We first consider a ball thrown up and against a wall, so that it bounces off the wall and returns to the pitcher, following the same path it took to the wall, but traversing that path in the reverse direction. Now consider the same experiment, swapping space and time so that the ball moves forward through time until encountering some obstacle, bounces and returns through increasingly earlier times, following the same path it took to the obstacle, but traversing the path in the reverse time direction. In order to sort out what this might mean, it is necessary to adopt the perspective of some observer who describes the two experiments using the space-time coordinates written (t,x) to signify an observed event at distance x made at time t in a particular laboratory. In the first experiment, a ball is thrown at time t_0 from position x_0 toward the wall (see Figure 1). At time t_1 the ball passes position x_1 on its way to the wall, and at time t_2 it hits the wall at position x_2. The ball reverses direction, so that at time t_3 it passes though position x_1 once again, heading back to the pitcher. Finally at time t_4 the ball returns to position x_0 where the pitcher stands. The observer records a sequence of events (position and time coordinates) that describe specific observations of the ball in its travels: (t_0,x_0), (t_1,x_1), (t_2,x_2), (t_3,x_1), (t_4,x_0). These coordinate observations correspond to our usual experience, as the time coordinate increases uniformly—t_0, t_1, t_2, t_3, t_4—while the space coordinate corresponds to the distance of the ball from the wall—decreasing from x_0, x_1, x_2 and then increasing back through x_1, x_0.

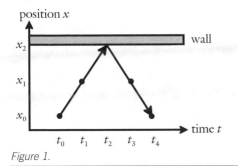

Figure 1.

Now, in the second experiment (see Figure 2), the ball is thrown at time t_0 from position x_0 toward the obstacle. At time t_1 it passes position x_1 on its way to the obstacle, and at time t_2 the ball hits the obstacle at position x_2. The ball reverses time direction, so that when it reaches position x_3 it is passing though time t_1 once again, heading backward in time. Finally, the ball reaches position x_4 as it returns to time t_0, the time at which it was thrown. As before the observer records a sequence of position and time coordinates that describe specific observations of the ball in its travels— (t_0,x_0), (t_1,x_1), (t_2,x_2), (t_1,x_3), (t_0,x_4).

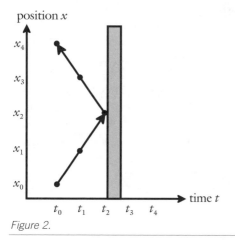

Figure 2.

But since the observer organizes the chronology of events according to the laboratory clock, two balls would initially appear, observed at (t_0,x_0) and at (t_0,x_4). The coordinates describe spatially separated observations of the ball—one at x_0 and one at x_4—but since both have the time coordinate t_0, they are described by the observer as occurring at the same time. Similarly, somewhat later at time t_1, the observer describes two spatially separated balls, one at x_1 and one at x_3. At time t_2 the observer sees the paths of the balls coincide at spatial coordinate x_2, and then at times t_3 and t_4, later than time t_2, the observer does not see the ball at all, anywhere. To this observer, it is as though two conventional balls of opposite nature travelled toward each other, met at the coordinates (t_2,x_2) and then disappeared. In particle physics, this process is called pair annihilation, and it has been routinely observed for more than 75 years, for example as the mutual annihilation of an electron and a positron (the anti-matter equivalent of the electron), emitting a burst of electromagnetic radiation. The first description of anti-matter as conventional matter travelling backward in time was given by Ernst Stueckelberg in the early 1940s, and was soon employed by Richard Feynman in elaborating the quantum theory of electrons.

The Feynman-Stueckelberg interpretation, as this understanding of time reversal has come to be called, has two obvious peculiarities. The observer, interpreting chronology according to the laboratory clock, simultaneously encounters the early history of the ball at (t_0,x_0) as it proceeds forward in time, and the late history of the ball at (t_0,x_4) as it proceeds backward toward earlier times. And to make sense of these observations, the observer interprets the two stages of the ball's motion as two independent objects (Figure 3) that meet coincidentally.

Anthropomorphizing a bit, suppose that a person could make a similar voyage, so that for example at age 53 I discover a technology that enables me to reverse the direction of my progress through time and return to the summer of 1967. By a somewhat fantastical extension of Stueckelberg's ideas, if I can travel backwards in time very quickly, I should find myself as a 53 year old in 1967 (not 13 as I was the last time I was there) with complete recall of the long strange trip leading first to the year 2007 and then back to the

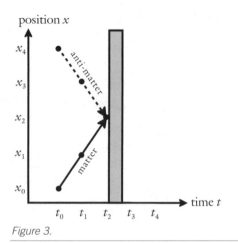

Figure 3.

earlier time. In fact, I should continue to age as the journey progresses, so that observers will notice a 13 year old slowing aging (if not maturing) while a certain old man gets progressively younger, until the pair meet at age 53 and then disappear. Presumably if time travel of this type were possible, it would have been observed already, as our descendents from the technologically advanced future come back to visit (I am grateful to my son Jonathan for this observation).

But in the Feynman-Stueckelberg interpretation, if there is truly a single ball observed at time t_0 both in its early history and in its late history, how do we distinguish these two moments physically, and more generally, how do we describe any alternative chronology of the ball's evolution through its historical stages?

Physicists refer to the observation of an object at a given location in space-time (the recording of its spatial and time coordinates) as an event. The sequence of observed events associated with a given object—its journey through space-time—is called a worldline, and the underlying physical process that produces the chronological sequence of events—drawing the worldline by incrementally morphing one event into a subsequent event—is called evolution. In this language, pair annihilation can be understood as the sequence of events observed in the laboratory reference frame when an evolving worldline reverses its direction in time. While the Feynman-Stueckelberg interpretation provides a compact explanation of pair annihilation, and is a significant component in quantum electrodynamics (QED), for which Feynman shared the 1965 Nobel Prize in physics with Julian Schwinger and Sin-Itiro Tomonaga, a number of questions remain open. How do we understand the chronology implied in describing the events on a worldline as constituting an ordered sequence, especially when it runs counter to the chronology recorded in a given reference frame? If it is reasonable to depict the events along a worldline as a chronological sequence of snapshots recording a single process that evolves from its internal past to its internal future, even when its internal future takes it into the laboratory observer's past, what parameter distinguishes and orders these events, and what is its physical status? Since the time measured by the clock on the laboratory wall is part of the observer's reference frame, it cannot provide this sequencing role, nor can it account for how an evolving entity would continue to age even as it returns to earlier laboratory times. Physicists have not reached at any well-founded consensus on a measurable candidate for an alternative chronological parameter. Most theoreticians consider the parameter to be unphysical, nothing more than an arbitrary assignment of numbers to the points along a line, and insist that a reasonable physical theory must be independent of how the parameter is chosen. On the other hand, Stueckelberg and others treat this evolution parameter as a physical time, coexisting with the four dimensions of space-time, and they divide the traditional roles of coordination and chronology between the two times. In this model, which I describe as I learned it from my teacher Lawrence P. Horwitz, who elaborated many of its essential features, the time measured on our clocks is called the Einstein time, signifies the time location of an object with respect to an arbitrary reference frame, and is subject to the restrictions on coordinate systems imposed by the principle of relativity. The Einstein time coordinate is associated with coordination behavior, as when we plan to meet at a certain hour and place, and measure our success by our simultaneous arrival at that space-time location. The evolution parameter is called the historical time, signifies the chronological evolution of events as they occur in historical sequence along the worldline, and is completely independent of the space-time coordinates. Evolving objects need not be "aware" of space and time—those quantities are assigned by observers working within their private reference frames—but they do "experience" the passage of a historical time that inexorably distinguishes its past from its future. In this language, a system behaves non-relativistically (like a classical Newtonian system) if the time coordinate is always identically equal to the historical time, always moving to later times and identical for all observers.

The basic observation that the two aspects of time can be assigned to physically separate measures and discussed independently, permits us to construct mathematically reasonable descriptions of what might otherwise become hopelessly confused narratives. Returning to pair annihilation, for example, the laboratory observer describes the seemingly unlikely process by which a particle and anti-particle ("coincidentally" the particle's mirror twin) follow symmetric paths "precisely constructed" so that they can meet and "combine" into a burst of energy. Although the anti-particle (the time reversed segment of the particle evolution as observed and ordered according to the laboratory clock) apparently adjusts its past so as to insure a pre-determined future, quantum electrodynamics explains that there are actually no miraculous coincidences in this story—only reinterpretation by the laboratory observer of the anti-particle's past and future. By distinguishing the anti-particle's historical past/future chronology from the coordinate past/future in a particular reference frame, the pair annihilation process becomes a causal sequence of events. While we have no well-established theory comparable to QED capable of giving empirically verifiable meaning to parallels in everyday human experience, one can conceivably make sense of such statements as "my entire past occurred as it did so as to lead me to this moment" if one is willing to claim that the causal chronology indeed occurred in reversed time as measured by our clocks. In other words, if "my past led to a pre-determined future" then it may be that my future occurred first chronologically, and I must explain, among other things, why I have not been observed to be getting younger as I evolve toward that chronologically earlier time. On the other hand, such a scenario is so completely speculative that the discussion is on no shakier ground if we consider processes in which the world-line evolves discontinuously, so that after advancing through my life in the usual forward time direction, I suddenly disappear from the shared present and appear in the past (or future) advancing again toward future times.

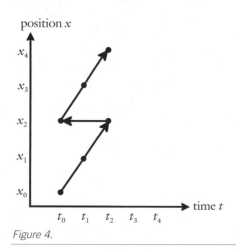

Figure 4.

Such parallels must accept the further implications of causality, meaning that however the events along my worldline are arrayed (whether I jump to the future or the past on some laboratory clock), the historical time determines a chronology that cannot be changed—I cannot affect the historical past. For example, in the pair annihilation experiment, I cannot force the anti-particle to miss the particle by grabbing the particle before they meet—since the worldline is one continuous sequence of events, if I remove the particle before the annihilation, the path of the anti-particle will never be created and the anti-particle will never be observed. Similarly, the so-called grandfather paradox—the objection to time travel on the grounds that one could change the past, and in the extreme case divert one's grandfather from the sequence of events that lead to one's birth—is absent in this formalism. The entire historical chronology that leads up to my travel back in time is a fait accompli before I visit my grandfather's youth, and whatever I do, I can only change the chronological future.

The difficulty in sorting out what time travel might involve can be reduced to the question of what physical interactions are possible, and to what degree they depend on separation in space-time versus separation in chronological time. Will 1967 be the way I remember it, or will I find that since the historical clock has continued ticking for everyone, therefore the 1967 of the historical now is different from the 1967 of the historical then? Will I be able to interact with anyone or anything, or will it turn out that I can only interact physically with objects at close values of the historical time, regardless of how close we may be in space-time? By analogy to the classical picture, shaking hands requires that a pair of hands arrive at about the same place at the same time, and if one hand arrives a few seconds too late to meet the other, the handshake can misfire. If physical interactions depend on a similar synchronization to the chronological time, then two hands attempting to shake at a certain space-time point, but arriving at very different historical times, will miss each other. As of now, the detailed understanding of these physical issues is extremely limited.

Stepping back from the most speculative issues, interesting applications of the concept of two times can be found in more modest questions about how we anticipate the future. First, the formalism discards the block universe and the coordinate abstraction, returning to a model in which, at any given moment of historical time, a group of related events is distributed across the spatial and temporal dimensions relevant to the problem at hand—a little to the right and a little to the left, a bit into the past, and a touch into the future. This distribution may undergo dynamic evolution as the historical time advances, first exhibiting a strong presence in one area of space-time, and later appearing in a different location. From this point of view, an observer who summarizes in an instant the totality of events that occur over the course of historical time will see the past and present coexist, separated in temporal distance, even though these events did not manifest themselves in the past and the present at the same historical moment. In the evolving space-time, the past exists only in memory, the future exists only in potential, and change is always possible.

Recalling the classical Newtonian picture, the coordinate time is always equal to the historical time, eliminating the bizarre possibility raised here that a chronologically future event will eventually manifest itself at our space-time location. Therefore, the equations of classical physics describe future conditions in some model based on past and present observations, and to the degree that a model is a correct and complete characterization of some empirical phenomenon, provides deterministic predictions of the world around us. Deterministic prediction of the future in the classical system is limited by the technical difficulty of constructing models, measuring present conditions in sufficient detail, and solving the equations that describe the model. For example, within the limits of classical physics, a ping-pong ball of known mass launched horizontally into a vacuum chamber with known initial velocity and height above the floor will land at the predicted location every time this experiment is repeated, but the landing place of the same ball launched into a high wind of rapidly changing intensity can only be effectively predicted if the wind speed and direction is known at each location of space and each moment of time. When the wind depends on the position of measurement but does not change over time at any given position—this is called the "static" case—

then accurate predictions can usually be made. On the other hand, if the time-dependence of the wind is not known a priori, then no exact prediction of the ping-pong ball's trajectory can be made before the time of its actual flight—the interaction that determines its path cannot be figured into a predictive calculation until it has manifested itself, and when the a posteriori calculation is compared with experiment, the word prediction is used in a figurative sense to mean reduction. But a rapidly changing wind can also complicate the task of extracting an a posteriori "prediction" from the mathematical model—finding an exact solution to Newton's laws for such a system may no longer be possible. Newton's laws associate changes in the physical interaction to changes in the geometrical configuration, and Newton's technique for solving them begins with a system in a known configuration and extrapolates the changes predicted by the model over a time period so short that even the simplest approximation to the model is sufficient. Extrapolating forward from the extrapolation, taking account of new values of the configuration and interaction at each step, the process continues until the system evolves to the present time. When the interaction is not too complicated, it changes in a predictable manner from one extrapolation to the next, and formal mathematical methods (calculus) provide an exact solution—the end result of this endless sequence of microscopic extrapolations—without needing to determine each intermediate step. But highly detailed and irregular interactions, such as a rapidly changing wind, usually make this kind of exact solution impossible to find, because the interaction changes significantly from one extrapolation to the next, rendering the formal techniques inapplicable. Approximate solutions may be found by programming a computer to emulate the intricate process of small extrapolations, or by defining a reasonable approximation to the interaction that admits a solution. When the actual phenomena are too complex to adequately measure and characterize, only an approximate model of interaction can be used, and science typically progresses from models of almost comic simplicity that mysteriously provide reasonable partial predictions of real situations, to increasingly sophisticated models that reflect greater insight into the important features of the underlying interactions. While it is tempting to rely on an approximate theory in the absence of an exact solution, based on partial observation or simplified characterization of real phenomena the value of the resulting predictions depends on the kind of approximation being made. While an exact solution can be found for the flight of a ping-pong ball by approximating the stormy wind as a soft and constant breeze, the resulting solution will probably deviate so strongly from the observed motion that the model may be less than useless—it will be misleading. Just such an approximation can be found, for example, in the popular prediction from the late 1990s, that the business innovations known as "the new economy" would guarantee uninterrupted economic growth into the 21st century and possibly indefinitely. This projection is mathematically equivalent to an exact solution to a Newtonian problem found using a simple approximation to a complex physical interaction, in this case, the simplistic assumption that the (often stormy) underlying relations of human society are essentially static (like a soft breeze) and can be simply extrapolated forward from their characterization in the mid-90s. As with the trajectory of the ping-pong ball in the wind, this assumption is sufficiently shaky to have rendered that prediction (observably) useless. On the other hand, predictions of global climate change are based on detailed models of incremental changes, analyzing in small steps how events in the recent past will affect emerging conditions in the short run, and then reapplying the technique to that outcome, analyzing how those future conditions, soon to be the recent past, will affect the next stage in an ongoing evolutionary drama. Because these climatic projections are obtained by following system changes one extrapolation at a time, they are less dependent on possible unknown variations in the underlying interactions.

Exact solutions for model processes are more difficult to obtain in post-Newtonian relativistic physics, because the rate of time passage becomes a dynamical quantity for the object in motion. In the two-time formalism, matters are complicated further because the coordinate time is on the same footing as spatial position, while the chronological time plays the role of time in Newtonian physics. By analogy to the Newtonian case, a static interaction is independent of the chronological time, but may depend on the coordinate time—such problems generally admit exact solutions. As in the Newtonian case, the difficult models involve non-static interactions, about which we may have limited a priori knowledge, and in this case, we may be able to predict observable conditions at any space-time point as they are affected up to the present chronological time, but can say nothing about unknown interactions in the chronological future. Thus, it becomes possible to state a prediction for future moments of coordinate time, subject to the caveat that the prediction is only valid in the present, meaning that before the future coordinate time can be observed, new interactions may occur to change that prediction. In some sense, we may form a very clear picture of the world in 2017, and yet this picture may appear entirely different when we reach the chronological 2017. An example of this kind of effect may be seen in the following model. Consider a process that sequentially launches ping-pong balls, one-by-one at a constant time interval, each horizontally and with the same initial velocity, into a time-varying horizontal wind. According to classical physics, each ball should land in a different location, because subsequent ping-pong balls experience different drag forces that affect the distance they cover before landing. But classically, the time of flight depends only on the initial height about the floor, and will be the same for every ping-pong ball—since the balls are launched at a constant time interval, they will land at a constant time interval. By tallying the number of ping-pong balls that land at each location, a distribution of landing places can be found. If the wind can be measured accurately, this distribution can be predicted deterministically by Newtonian theory. In the two-time relativistic picture, ping-pong balls launched at a constant interval of historical time will land at the same constant interval of historical time, and the distribution of space-time landing places can be tallied. In some cases, balls landing at different historical times will arrive at the same spatial location at the same coordinate time. At any given historical time, the model will provide a partial tally of ping-pong balls landing at a given time coordinate, reflecting the landing events up to that moment in historical time, and if we do not tally ping-pong balls sufficiently long, we may undercount the eventual number of arrivals at that time coordinate. In everyday language, this means that a physically reasonable theory, capable in principle of predicting what will happen in an hour, may provide explicit forecasts of no practical value, because the final result is excessively sensitive to events that will not have begun for another 59 minutes. In such a theory, causality remains deterministic, but there is room for sufficient dynamic variation to make any advance prediction of outcomes impractical. In order to make reliable predictions from a physical model in the two-time formalism, it is necessary to understand how the mechanisms by which the system evolves from moment to moment in chronological time, and have sufficiently detailed knowledge of the dependence of the underlying interaction on chronological time and on the space-time locations of the interacting elements. Bringing these requirements into everyday experience, any attempt at an explanation of observed phenomena requires that we understand how the relationships among the participants induce microscopic evolution over very short historical times, how those relationships depend on the spatial and temporal separation of the participants, and how the relationships themselves may change as chronological time advances. Since most of this information is not available for social interactions, this discussion primarily indicates a possible framework for speculation representing a level of freedom of thought similar to what "hard science" permits to itself.

We seem to be on the brink of talking about human language. The internet is an interesting place to begin, because in some ways it is not a good example of human discourse, and many commentators would be surprised at the suggestion that the typical exchange of views on an internet forum is less one-sided than a conversation with the dead. That remark may seem uncharitable, given the nature of our project and the fact that the internet underlies my main means of support, and no disrespect is intended toward the medium or the technology. My point is that the internet represents an abstraction and generalization of older forms of human communication, ranging from arts and letters to graffiti, so that while it offers new approaches to creative interaction through language, it also permits other forms of linguistic expression less associated with discourse than with vandalism. The concern you express for face-to-face encounters is well placed and precisely relevant here—many writers have returned to this issue recently as a starting point for understanding the negative side of the networked interaction, from the inextinguishable flame wars (abusive messages posted to discussion groups and "talkback" pages of online newspapers) to internet-based stalking, bullying, slander, and extortion. Internet discourse is a new form of "virtual communication" mediated by a network of computers through a human-machine interface, and for some people the experience of interacting directly with a machine, rather than another human being, interferes with this abstract model of human-to-human contact. Older examples of this interference are known from the telephone, which conveys a disembodied voice without any nonverbal cues from the human partner. Many people are reticent about speaking on the phone without these cues, and experience an odd sensation when hearing a familiar voice distorted by the low fidelity of telephone transmission, or an urge to shout on long distance calls, despite the generally reasonable audio volume and low noise level on contemporary phone lines. While many internet users manage to push the intermediary machine into the background and focus on the human interaction, others apparently do not, and in the absence of immediate human cues and meta-language, abandon the self-restraint they may bring to their face-to-face interactions, leading to a verbal analog of road rage. Besides the problem of good web citizens allowing their manners to slip when no one is present to hint at what is expected, the vision of an efficiently networked, direct democracy of immediate individual participation is not universally shared. To many, the internet embodies a fragmented and alienated society, where thousands are whispering and no one is listening—the millions of personal blogs uploaded every day produce a mountain of undifferentiated factoids that very few actually read, and no one can possibly integrate. The difficulty of being heard in this information glut, together with the perceived anonymity of internet conversation emboldens some to vent anti-social thoughts and feelings they otherwise keep private. Against this background, by asking how the participants in an internet-based democracy can impose individual self-restraint or new legal structures that will preserve the collective interest, you raise a serious concern. On the other hand, humans have shown an ability to disregard the collective interest and the humanity of others even in the presence of direct face-to-face communication, so while the internet may conceivably evolve into a significant instrument of harm, at the present time the dangers it presents reflect those conventional problems.

As you pointedly observe, even to the extent that the internet forms a democracy of expression, it cannot by itself provide any redistribution of political or economic power. Despite the myth floating around cyberspace for the past twenty years that envisions a major shift in economic power as information capital is shared and downloaded by every potential entrepreneur, much as music and video recordings are shared today, no evidence for such a transition has been seen. The dialectical struggle between traditional conceptions of "intellectual property" and the technology of digital storage and reproduction is primarily about how "intellectuals"—and the businesses that support them—should be compensated for their work. While the internet has made the traditional distribution and unit pricing of books and recordings obsolete, information capital is fundamentally different because entrepreneurial secrets are not intended for wide-scale sharing and distribution in the first place. It is one thing for the buyer of a recording to make a reproduction generally available at zero cost, and quite another to openly share potentially valuable information, even if not bound by nondisclosure agreements.

The answer you give to your larger question of whether the internet can be a "place of significant formation of personal identities" seems to me again to rest on abstractions from earlier forms of human communication. To the extent that the network enables communication with physically distant correspondents, helps us reestablish lapsed relationships, enhances our powers of memory, and provides us with artifacts from younger times, it is a kind of power tool for recreating identity in the traditional sense. Again, the very description of the internet as a "place" (whether a mere "information superhighway" or a full-fledged "cyberspace") has a fascinating history, but is of course a metaphorical reference to older ways of thinking about face-to-face social relations. The actual internet, an assemblage of computer hardware and software, may provide us with an experience reminiscent of place, but only for those of us who prefer to imagine communication as happening in a place. The phrase "chat room" can make the web seem friendlier to an older age cohort (to me it conjures up visions of a bath house), but my personal impression is that the generation that has grown up with email, chat, SMS, and mobile telephony has no need for these euphemisms—they simply regard human communication as naturally taking place across a wide scale of time and distance. In this way, the internet allows us to form social identities with groups of people that could not practically assemble in one place, and it is these actual social interactions, albeit mediated and shifted in time and space, that can become part of identity. I have no doubt that some people see themselves entering cyberspace to meet with a reference group that truly resides in that ethereal other-world, just as I have met people who fully believe that they physically reside in Woodstock Nation or the Merry Old Land of Oz. This tendency to enhance the reality of the most imaginary aspect of the imagined community, while diminishing the reality of the actual community is also not unique to the internet.

So, in relation to language, the internet is interesting because it provides a medium of human exchange so rich and inclusive that we are temped to endow the process of internet communication with the significance of community, identity, polity, and locality, and yet that process highlights certain aspects of face-to-face human conversation precisely because it is not the same. In direct conversation, both consideration and convention prescribe that the listener show attentiveness to the speaker through listening behaviors that effectively constitute a nonverbal or partially verbal form of simultaneous speaking. By acknowledging the spoken message in this way, the listener provides the speaker a degree of confidence in the mutual comprehension and overall success of the communication, helping to establish a mutually coherent experiential context for the conversation. But mechanically mediated communication, whether a conventional letter or internet chat, shifts the message through time and space, generally restricting or eliminating parallel listening behavior, and leaving both speaker and listener essentially free to invent a pair of possibly distinct contexts, recalling the warmth of a face-to-face conversation or the indifference of reviewing a laundry list. So while a love letter is best written and read as though the partner were immediately present, a mortgage foreclosure may be written without any consideration of a human recipient and read in a tone not likely addressed directly to the banker. A gripping example of these possibilities appeared in the film *Apocalypse Now*; a young soldier is unexpectedly killed while listening to a tape-recorded message from his mother, and his comrades look on in horror as she lovingly urges him to be careful and return home safely. Similarly, but more than any previous form of machine-mediated communication, the internet decouples, in both space and time, the process of speaking from the process of listening, while permitting a high degree of immediacy and richness. The construction of cultural meanings— community, identity, place—surrounding the act of internet communication, is a natural and unsurprising aspect of human behavior, but (as the anthropologist who has been to law school pointedly observes) none of this provides "a distribution of power, that is of the means of coercion, commensurate with the distribution of the means of articulation."

Engineers describe the computers that create the internet experience as intermediary messengers communicating among one another, and again the uniqueness of human language is highlighted by the fundamentally different methods used by these machines to exchange information. Benveniste's central argument is that among all the nouns and pronouns, the words "I" and "You" are unique, in that they do not indicate a fixed referent, but rather identify a pair of individuals in the act of defining a relationship between them. Moreover, unlike other words, the antecedent references of the first and second person pronouns change as speaker and listener exchange roles within this relationship, and are understood solely from context by the acts of speaking and listening. For Benveniste, the invocation of the pronoun "I" is then the defining act of personhood—the individual integrating separate experiences into a "psychic unity" with a "permanence of consciousness", distinguished from otherness by the defining act of invoking the word "You." When denoting entities outside of this polarized relationship of first and second person, we speak in the third person of nouns and pronouns that have fixed referents. Language is thus characterized by the human ability to distinguish the referent for first and second person pronouns from context, and while it is not entirely clear that no machine can have this ability, computers operating over the internet do not function this way. Since computers can be easily programmed to associate symbolic references with physical relationships, internet machines refer to themselves and to each other in the third person, using the fixed names and addresses assigned to them, directly or indirectly, by human administrators. Similarly unlike human speech, the different aspects of a computer's "personality" and "experience" remain fragmented, with various capabilities operating independently in separate programs. In some cases, such as web browsing, most personal computers can initiate internet communication, but cannot respond to reciprocal initiatives from other computers. For example, home computers can visit remote web sites, but typically have no web site of their own for others to visit, and no facility to provide remote access to such a site if it existed—web sites are generally "hosted" on computers specifically configured to provide that service. In other cases, initiative and response are handled separately, so that the user's email program must send and receive email via distinct software entities that often operate by connecting to different remote machines. The computer's software-based abilities are usually divided into Client programs that request and accept service from other programs (often at the behest of a user), and Server programs that accept these requests and provide an appropriate service. At the human level, when Martin at computer A sends email to Jonathan at computer B containing the line "I am happy to speak to you" and Jonathan replies, "And I am happy to speak to you," we easily sort out the meaning of the words "I" and "You" in this polar relationship from context. But, even in the simplest case in which both computers handle their own email delivery (without relying on external email service providers, as most private internet users must do), the relay of the messages and reply involves six steps among four connected but independently functioning software entities (Figures 5 and 6):

1. Martin's computer speaks to Jonathan's computer saying, "Message from email Client at computer A to email Server at computer B"

2. Jonathan's computer speaks to Martin's computer saying, "Acknowledgement of message delivery from email Server at computer B to email Client at computer A"

3. The email Server at computer B forwards Martin's message to the email Client at computer B so Jonathan can read it

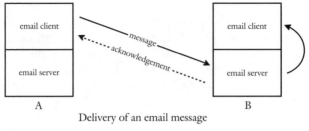

Delivery of an email message

Figure 5.

---

4. Jonathan's computer speaks to Martin's computer saying, "Message from email Client at computer B to email Server at computer B"

5. Martin's computer speaks to Jonathan's computer saying, "Acknowledgement of message delivery from email Server at computer A to email Client at computer B"

6. The email Server at computer A forwards Jonathan's reply to the email Client at computer A so Martin can read it

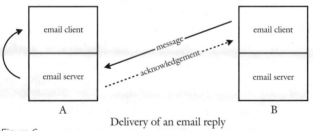

Delivery of an email reply

Figure 6.

These features of the internet—the division of client and server functions into separate software entities and the consistent use of third person identification—are not necessary requirements of machine communication, but are intended to make the internet a robust "open system" in which machines can communicate without any prior formal acquaintance. Many common systems function by invoking first and second person formulations, so that for example, if Martin's computer and Jonathan's computer have been properly introduced to one another, they can exchange email messages by respectively announcing, "I have an email message for you," and "I have a reply message for you." In that case, in any message arriving on a network cable, the word "I" refers to the sender and "You" refers to the software that accepts the message, while the opposite associations hold for messages leaving on the network cable. Nevertheless, it would be an unreasonable stretch to argue that the computer invoking the word "I" has unified its fragmented experience into a consistent subjective ego.

Unlike normal face-to-face conversation, you and I have been conducting this discussion by writing long email messages that "speak" an extended discourse at once, and similarly replying with an extended response all at once. For the usual reasons associated with face-to-face conversation, the internet computers that relay the email generally divide the message into smaller pieces that are sent and acknowledged as separate messages. Like the speaker in direct conversation, the "speaking" computer has no difficulty simultaneously sending the message and receiving the acknowledgement messages from the "listening" computer (the listening behavior). In fact, unlike most humans, computers can simultaneously send and receive independent messages and their associated acknowledgements—four simultaneous streams of speech. Engineers distinguish two kinds of bi-directional communication: full-duplex systems permit the simultaneous transfer of information in two directions, while half-duplex systems permit information to flow in only one direction at a time, first in one direction, and then the other. So, while modern computers are generally full-duplex systems in exchange of content and acknowledgements, face-to-face conversation can manage full-duplex operation at the level of speaking and acknowledgement (because it is asymmetric, with acknowledgements flowing at a much lower information transfer rate than content), but is generally half-duplex at the level of speaking and speaking—most of us cannot express thoughtful content and simultaneously listen to another do the same. Although chat and email are full-duplex systems in principle, their use is effectively limited to half-duplex, because the spatial and temporal separation of writer and reader makes reply impossible until the message arrives. An underlying technical feature of the service provided by the network, involving the level of connectivity between mediating computers, affects how users experience the half-duplex relationship. In systems that engineers call connectionless service, content messages are sent without prior agreement from the recipient, proceeding by "best effort" delivery (meaning no guarantee and no acknowledgment of actual delivery). Conventional mail and email are connectionless systems—no prior arrangements need be made before sending mail, no guarantee of actual delivery is offered by the system, and the sender has no information about the message status until a return message is received from the recipient. Connection-oriented service on the other hand is like a conventional telephone call, requiring the recipient to accept the call, thereby acknowledging delivery and providing a greater experience of immediacy for the caller. Unlike email, which arrives unannounced, the connection-oriented chat system requires that the network provide an active communications channel to the participants for the duration of the session, just as a telephone connection remains active for the duration of a call, even when no one is speaking in words.

Reading the quotation from Edmond Jabès entirely out of context—I was not able to find the reference—my first reaction was to ask what level of silence he regards as having the power to push him from the present into the past, and my second reaction was to ask what it means to say, "I was." Approaching the first question conservatively, I thought of a phone call, in which we normally take turns speaking and listening, but remain in a relationship of communication, and in that sense not silent, until one of us actively ends the connection. This approach seems to me conservative because the decision by a living partner to preserve the connection despite the death of another partner, allows for "a living relationship with the dead," without appealing to any pre-Enlightenment lifeworld, but remains agnostic as to whether and in what sense the dead speak back to us. By understanding the continuation of relationship as the negation of silence, the question of who is speaking as "I" becomes unimportant to the argument—both partners are, regardless of which speaker experiences the birth of a coherent ego by invoking the word "I" and which one experiences the shining light of recognition by being addressed as "You." It is something of a platitude that when we speak of the dead in the third person, we keep their memory and significance alive. Although this interpretation of Jabès seems minimally consistent and may even satisfy Walter Benjamin, it does not take into account the quotation's direct address to us in the second person, and the expectation that we will reply by addressing the speaker equally directly. Even the post-Enlightenment thinkers among us who insist that the basic condition of being for the dead is complete absence of consciousness, corporeal coherence, and activity, must admit that we become the second person and listen to the dead, when we accept messages they recorded when they were alive. Modern conceptions of time further permit us to speculate that, just as letters and internet messages are received through a forward shift in time and space, perhaps some process enables messages to be transmitted backward in time, so that in the past my father "heard" the message created by my thinking of him now (in what was then the future). The second question is more difficult, because death, time, and past tense are not equivalent, despite the use of the past tense as a euphemism. In any lifeworld, unless we want to drain any possible meaning from the word death, we must agree that there are qualities we associate with living people and not with the dead, whether or not participating in first person conversations is among them. Wishing to avoid the well-known grammatical conundrums exposed by analytical philosophy, I do not want to discuss the ontology of "having been" at length, any more than I want to get bogged down in the ontology of "I am not." However, from a purely grammatical point of view, the statement, "I was" is true for the living as well as the dead, because if the statement "she is" implies life, then the statement, "she is dead" cannot be parsed. Moreover, when we refer to the dead in the past tense, we mean that they were alive in the past, not that they themselves remain in the past, like temporal lost luggage or whatever else that might mean. The discussion ultimately returns to the ancient difficulty of comprehending how a person can be born, live, and then die, continuing to exist among us as a dead person about whom we still experience relationship, feelings, memories, and other forms of lasting material and spiritual influence. So before we try to understand the ontological status of an entirely extinct humanity, let us first consider the more normal condition of those who have been dead long enough that no one alive remembers them personally and no one speaks to them (or says *kaddish* for them). If Jabès is right then such a person indeed "was" and "is not" in much the same physical manifestation as "will be" applied before being born. So, to invoke a communications-related euphemism from a different milieu, if humanity becomes extinct, then that's all she wrote, and we will be gone as if we had never been, and it will not matter to a single person. Perhaps, by some clever *pilpul* (line of reasoning) involving the terms of the covenant, or by an argument about God needing listeners in order to exist Himself, you, like Abraham at Sodom or perhaps more like Portia at Venice, will eventually cancel the decree and convince Him that He cannot allow us to commit ecocide. However, it seems to me that the recognition that God "is the partner who makes it possible for us to be so long as we are listeners" is not a new idea—it is precisely the part of the covenant that we have so often ignored to our peril. If we were listening to God, then we would be treating one another, and the earth itself along with the other species who share it with us, with greater respect and we would recognize the divine imperative of radically changing our collective behavior in order to prevent the oncoming cataclysm. It is interesting in this context to notice that we have focused here on ways in which speaking is connected to the subjective experience of ego and to preservation of memory, while listening—in the sense of the Hebrew *shema*, hear and obey—is connected to our experience of ourselves as objective, collective, and productive. It is then not surprising that analysis of how language functions (such as Chomskian grammar) usually begins with the facility of comprehension of language in the listener, and deals with speakers as builders of messages that listeners can understand. It was in this context that the talk I heard by Julia Kristeva came to mind. She spoke of the experience of being a refugee and the importance in her life of having been offered hospitality (political asylum), and said that she had come to regard hospitality as the elementary act of humanity. Thinking of her statement in light of Benveniste, and formalizing the idea of hospitality through the literal meaning of such formulas as "me casa su casa" and "ahalan wa-sahalan," it occurred to me that we can describe the act of yielding the role of first person and offering that position to the friend, stranger, or refugee, to whom we listen attentively, as a basic act of hospitality and humanity. Elsewhere ("The Other Language or the Condition of Being Alive") she has said,

> Hospitality is not only the simple juxtaposition of differences with one model dominating all the others, and feigning respect for others whilst really being indifferent towards them. On the contrary, hospitality is a real attempt to understand other kinds of freedom in order to make every "way of being" more multiple, more complex. The definition of humanity that I was looking for is perhaps just this process of complexification.

So conversely, to truly listen is to understand other kinds of freedom or "I"-ness.

But if indeed the lights never dimmed on Broadway throughout the Final Solution, and you see in this a parallel to the current lack of significant movement toward avoiding global environmental catastrophe, then I do not see a problem of inflection between past and future tense, but rather a typically human example of learning from experience to make a prediction that may well be ignored despite its value. I suppose that the banal lack of difficulty we have in imagining such a catastrophe explains why the word "ecocide" appears in the spell-checker of my word processor. Similarly, I cannot see any escape or even comfort in the recognition that the concept of the present is essentially grammatical and not ontological—the prediction remains. As Benveniste observes, the past and future are distinguished because they are separated by the present, and the present "has only a linguistic fact as temporal reference: the coincidence of the event described with the instance of discourse that describes it." In other words, the act of speaking designates a particular point in chronological time as the present just as it designates the speaker as "I" and the listener as "You", but the arbitrariness of "now" does not eliminate chronology or erase our understanding of how one thing leads to another. If I observe two events occurring one after the other, I can wait some time and describe both as having occurred in the past, or if I speak coincidentally with the second event I can describe the first event as having occurred in the past and the second as occurring in the present. Whatever may occur subsequent to my speaking is a future event, about which my knowledge is limited by my ability to predict the underlying dynamics that affect it. But "being" is something else, expressing the continuous evolution of a consistent entity through chronological time, even if that entity represents an extended object that ceases to act in a coherent manner and disperses over large distances (that is, it dies). In this sense, Jabès is describing all possible presents, meaning all possible times up to the present (as fixed by my writing this sentence) that could potentially have been chosen as the present moment by annunciating then that "You are silent, I was; you speak, I am." And so having built horribly complicated definitions, we return to the ancient realization that the past represents the events we can possibly have observed and recorded in memory before the moment of our speaking, the present represents the events that occur as we speak, and the future is unknown but subject to prediction. And that prediction is infuriatingly difficult to make, because we can never understand the underlying dynamics of our evolution well enough, or make all the required observations to extrapolate forward, and our observed present may yet be affected by events from the chronological future. That difficulty may lessen the despair of certain catastrophe and allow us to live in hope, but whether we choose to impose on the uncertain future a positive or negative face, what is coming will be the consequence of what happens now. This applies equally to global warming and the eventual table of contents of this book, and of course my list was somewhere between a suggestion and a prediction, with no intention of imposing—bullet points blazing—a future to be fulfilled at all cost.

The idea of returning to small, local, face-to-face interactions as a way to avert climate change does not seem practical for several economic reasons, some reasonable and some not. Since the liberal vision of global economy places no particular value on locality as such, when the cost of transport is smaller than the differential in production costs in remote markets, import/export wins. Making transportation costs reflect the damage to the environment, which does not affect the worst sources of pollution, would probably enhance locality by reducing trade. But trade is not merely about finding the cheapest source of running shoes, it is also about having something to eat besides a monoculture of yams or corn or whale blubber or cactus fruit, depending on which "village model" you happen to be stuck in. And so, to the extent that globalization increases opportunity and choice by enlarging the circle of exchange, most people seem to approve, while opposition is provoked when the power of mass marketing and economies of scale restrict choice, eliminating jobs, markets, local culture and traditional ways of living. It would probably be more precise to say that globalization is not the problem at all, except when used as a euphemism for the nasty habit of capitalism to enforce homogeneity. Thus, when the symbols of globalization are Zabar's, Balducci's, Ikea, and Vermont maple syrup on the grocery shelves in Umm El-Fahm, we do not hear much complaining. But when locally made organic peanut butter cannot compete with the well-known American brand, the local shops disappear because transnational chains are turning the world into a strip mall, and corporate lenders condition foreign investment on the elimination of otherwise successful local business practices, the homogenizing force of the global market makes its victims aware of "alien" influence. The resistance to homogenizing globalization is usually associated with the third world and certain parts of Europe, but is occurring at the time of this writing in New York City as Wal-Mart—the corporation most admired by Wall Street—attempts to bring its Dickensian union-busting practices to Manhattan. But among the emotions generated by globalization, the most powerful and least addressed feeling is our anger at our cohabitants in the village, the people like us who make homogeneity possible by preferring the uniform import to the local variation. I am not surprised when McDonalds in downtown Jerusalem attracts tourists in baseball caps, Bermuda shorts, and Gap T-shirts, preferring a familiar experience to foreign cuisine, but I find it demoralizing that it is usually filled with second and third generation Israelis from the diasporas of Morocco, Yemen, and Poland in baseball caps, Bermuda shorts, and Gap T-shirts, super-sizing themselves as they begin what George Carlin called "slow death by fast food." It seems that very few of us feel much sense of significant loss at local traditions disappearing, at old shuls closing down, ethnic restaurants becoming chain stores, and scholarly traditions being forgotten. When we feel that loss, we talk about community and continuity, even when a community of shared values refers to six people spread over three continents building a locality on the internet. Homogeneity seems to be quite welcome in much of the world, and until it becomes xenophobia, we seldom hear criticism of globalization from the traditional isolationist viewpoint that fears foreign entanglement. It would have actually been an encouraging sign if prominent Americans had argued in 2002 that by invading Iraq, the US was getting in over its head, and picking a fight with forces that are too foreign to understand and too powerful to overcome. All in all, it seems that place is in the past.

thln_005 (Jonathan)

As I wrote to you immediately after receiving thln_004 (an unconscionably long time ago, except for our original agreement that we would set no deadlines in this exchange), I was thrilled to receive so many words, both because I always enjoy any chance I have to push you to explain your physics to me, and more immediately because I seemed to have succeeded in provoking you to write most of this book.

I am a bit stymied (or was, until I resolved to commence by stating "I am a bit stymied") not by a poverty of matter for response, but by a formal dilemma. "Your" thln_004 evokes less a series of new meditations in me for which it would provide the trajectory, than a series of interrogations that burrow into thln_004 at various points. The form of the gloss would be most apt here, though it is likely unfeasible. In this, nevertheless, I/Jonathan act to some extent as stand-in for me/the reader who is to come, predicting, based on my response, at least some of what will have been difficult in your text for another reader.

Provisionally, therefore, at least most of this text, thln_005, is doubly keyed back to thln_004: first by page numbers which simply refer to a Word file as printed in hard copy; and second to phrases appearing on those respective pages. We will, *insh'allah*, eventually resolve the practical task of reworking this "citation format" in a way that also invites you, the reader who is neither Martin nor Jonathan. (I suppose I had always read Jabès' "You are silent, I was; you speak, I am" as addressed to me, to Jonathan, not in the moment of the author's writing or the volume's printing but in the moment of my, Jonathan's, reading.)

Thus:

Page 28:

"irresistible anxiety:" You apologize for doing what I have, after all, been asking you to do for years. Why does this produce "irresistible anxiety" in you (an anxiety, it seems, at having written which we might contrast to the anxiety of not having written)? Are you anxious that there will be no "reception," as might or might not be the case were you delivering a lecture to a room full of hundreds of people, and you would have almost no way to know; or are you anxious that there will be no "dialogue," that you will not be nourished in return? Are these the same anxiety?

Page 29:

"how objects are separated in space-time:" Recently, along with neighbors, Elissa and I made our annual trip up to our Manhattan rooftop to see the July 4 Macy's fireworks: Some shapes: a smiley face, a heart... and most stunning, a series of red cubes of light high above the East River. This firework ritual is the cyclical invocation and obliteration of history and yet, perhaps, a linear story of promise fulfilled is also told as each year the fireworks become "better."

"physical influence:" What does "physical" mean? Are we (Martin, Jonathan, the reader yet to be named) interacting objects? What is the difference to "God" between "objects" and "frames of reference?"

Page 30:

"The causal principle:" Just to underscore (since I had to reread and reread here): coordinate time is clock time (as it seems here); "historical time" is not "clock time," contrary to what I persisted in assuming (vigilant as I always am to detect and denounce historians' notion of homogeneous, empty time that is filled with events; a vigilance that might of course shape what it sees in the image of its own spectral fears).

"it may be possible to 'travel backward in time':" But how could we "appear" without changing time? [The solution adopted by the *Back to the Future* movie trilogy, brilliant for its dramatic purposes, is to mark only certain, presumably life-transforming events (an ancestor not meeting her mate) as risking a "fundamental disruption of the space-time continuum."] What, in any case, would "we" be?

Page 31:

"The projected contents may be... entirely correct:" I am reminded of a slogan I saw last month, projected on an electronic announcement board in the train station at Lausanne: "We don't have to predict the future; we just have to make it possible." Should I regard this as trivial, as necessarily a meliorative moralism for capitalism because found in a major train station, not merely unattributed but moreover alternating with other, more obviously banal slogans? Or dare I risk validating it, on the grounds (say) that this was the country of Einstein and Paul Klee? At least it echoes forward to a question below, namely, why the difficulty of predicting the future should be "agonizing" to us.

Page 32:

"*I make no other claim for the value of these notions*:" Why adopt such a limited view of science? Is science a culprit here? How is science something separate? Are you arguing for a renewed respect for "our wider intuitive understandings of place and temporality" (earlier in this same paragraph)?

Page 35:

"*to explain a ball falling from our hand*:" I am on uncertain ground and intrigued here. When you write, "in this spirit," it seems to me (now, on rereading) you are referring to the "spirit" of a Cartesian-coordinate imagination in which we talk about *effects* of *forces* on discrete objects, rather than about dynamic *processes* that affect manifestations (or events) as "objects" in the universe. Tell me if this is right, for if not, I risk continuing onto a path of ridiculousness, ignoring your caution at page 32 above by enthusiastically analogizing your scientific discussion to a human social one. But I do risk it, for the analogy is too tempting to this analytic distinction in ways of talking about human events. One way of talking is to take the objects (religions, ethnicities) as givens and to talk about forces that affect them; the other is to talk about the processes that produce the "religion effect" or "the history effect." The latter strikes me as both more compelling and more promising for the prospects of discourse aiding us in our attempt to survive. Stanley Diamond said something like this (albeit more concretely) decades ago:

> For example, in this perspective the modern world, through the interaction of the major states, may be viewed as responsible for Stalinism, not the evil

genius of the Russian people, not domestic Soviet events alone, nor the abstract compulsions of a particular version of "Marxism." In the same way, our civilization is responsible for Nazism, not the constitutional perfidy of the Germans, etc.

In the same way, though I think guilt is not called for here, the evident degradation of our immediate future prospects is not *someone else's fault*.

Page 37:

"*Einstein's relativity principle requires...*:" What does it mean to "choose" among the four axes of space-time? Is an "axis" of space-time the same thing as a dimension? Also, what implications of the foregoing sentence lead to the "Consequently" that begins the next sentence?

Page 38:

"*This fixed universe must then either extend infinitely into the future, or lead to some moment at which time ends*:" How, precisely, is this temporal characteristic of Einstein's "fixed" or "block" universe viewed differently or critiqued in a two-timing physics? What does it mean for time to end? Is the attempt to conceive that any more difficult for us than the notion of space ending at a certain point in a fixed universe? Can we really talk about time ending?

Page 42:

"*[I]f time travel of this type were possible*:" I am reminded, first, of something you said to me in our college days—that history really should make as much sense going backward as well as forward. This has stood me well, and in fact much of my ethnography *Polish*

Jews in Paris was an effort to tell the history of a generation of immigrants backward from the time of my fieldwork encounter with them. More personally, I have occasionally speculated, or tried to comfort myself, with the thought that the past is such a rich country I need not sorrow overmuch as my personal future or the world's shrinks in relation to that past that remains infinitely discoverable. Yet such thoughts seem unworthy historicist self-numbings, precisely the nostalgic temptation Walter Benjamin warned against. Should they be banned as an estheticization of history, inimical to its real politicization? Or should we historicize Benjamin as well, noting the desperation that led to his bombastic rhetoric about taking a "tiger's leap into the past," avoiding "historicism's bordello," and being "man enough to blast open the continuum of history?" If we criticize him less because of the desperation of his circumstances, how shall be evaluate the desperation of our own?

You speak of an "observer... simultaneously encounter[ing]" the same object as it moves forward and backward in time. But how could the observer be in only one time (presumably, the time moving forward) and "encounter" (be, that is, in some way co-present with) something moving backward in time as well? Put another way: How can you be in two times at once (when you're not any time at all)? From the observer's perspective ("interpreting chronology according to the laboratory clock") the "two stages" seem independent objects. But here, it seems, you are once again in the habit of speaking independently of the observer and the ball, rather than the process that relates them. Since we are in the habit of imagining our thinking, discursive "selves" in the place of this observer, it is especially hard to shake that habit in a scenario such as this one. So a difficult question might be, what is the relation between the observer and the ball in its two stages?

In the rest of page 42, you do indeed "anthoropomorphiz[e quite] a bit." Isn't the real problem with time travel (dependent, as it is, on the positing of a traveler who somehow remains sufficiently coherent to remain identifiable at both time initial time *y* and (logically posterior, but chronologically either anterior or posterior) time *x*) its reliance on a fantastically problematical reification of ego—not the unidirectionality of time but the linearity (or better, the evolutionary nature) of selfhood?

Perhaps our descendants "from the technologically advanced future" have no need or interest in visiting us; or perhaps they have come to visit, but there was no one home.

"*Physicists refer to the observation of an object at a given location in space-time... as an event:*" I have gotten somewhat used (with thanks/acknowledgments, I'm not sure where or why, to Judith Butler) to thinking of each human being (and, I suppose, and to anticipate your argument further down, the species itself) as an "event." But by your definition ("Physicists refer... ") it would not be me, but rather only me here and now, that is the event. This seems to imply that, if I want somehow to comfort myself and others by naming the boundedness of myself and the species, I need some term other than "event." What shall that be?

Page 45:

[Interruption: listening to a tape given to me by my rabbi (!) of a recent live concert by the Allman

Brothers, the first track is the lead-in or first measures of "Jessica." Slightly slower than on the original album recording, to which I was listening as I drove my parents' red Opal a few days after I'd gotten my driver's license, west on West Park Avenue toward Campbell's Lake with L—V—, tremendously happy, missed a stop sign at a time when a car (invisible around the intersection anyway) was coming through which rear-ended my car and sent it spinning and, though no one was hurt, still leaves me with the almost unshakeable impression that this closest connection of my life until then was poisoned by that moment.]

"While we have no well-established theory…:" Is the situation in which "my future occurred first chronologically" any different from a narrative (which remains difficult in fact to conceive, let alone to articulate) of history starting with the present and going backward? Does our common predilection for seeing ourselves growing older rather than younger cause our tendency to see the past moving into the future? Why do we think we know the past better than the future—merely because our observations about the past accord better with the observations of others than our observations about the future? Why does the "young" Dylan's line "I was so much older then, I'm younger than that now" affect us so powerfully? Why do we think we know what that line means but have such a hard time glossing it? I do think I understand, from your account of Stueckelberg's notion of historical sequence, why "I cannot affect the historical past" (which is presumably why the dramatic-tension premises of *Back to the Future* were so unconvincing if you thought about them hard enough).

Page 48:

　　"In the evolving space-time, the past exists only in memory, the future exists only in potential, and change is always possible:" Does the confusion lie in the common tendency to think of going back into the past as going back "in history," whereas you are saying that even if you could move in either direction along the temporal dimension of a fixed universe, "historical" time only moves forward? I think so. Yes, this does seem to be what you are saying here.

　　About a week ago my son Jonah reported to me that, as he was drifting off to sleep, he thought of writing his "memoirs"—the account of an entire life—now, based on memory up until the present and constructed "fictionally" from this present on.

Page 51:

　　The notion of a prediction about the future that is "only valid in the present" seems important for the ethics of projection. In a simple sense, it weakens the force of propaganda aimed at foreclosing present action based on plausible projections of catastrophic climate degradation; that propaganda is, by your formulation, more clearly shown to rest on the slim reed of the possibility that things might not turn out *to have been* so disastrous (and thus that there would have been no necessity to interfere with the profit motive), not that they are *unlikely to be* disastrous. Similarly, and perhaps also commonsensically, it reinforces our responsibility to act in the face of uncertainty according to our *best understanding* of our present choice of actions and their various likely outcomes. That our best understanding might (as you point out) just not be good enough hardly reduces our responsibility for the future *now*.

Page 52:

"*[A] physically reasonable theory...:*" Your point that a prediction of the way things will be in an hour might be perfectly valid for the first 59 minutes of that hour calls to mind Mathieu Kassovitz's film *La Haine*. An initial voice-over tells the old joke about the man who falls from a high building and, as he passes each floor on his descent, calls out "So far, so good!" We the viewers should have been forewarned by that story, but none of us believed that the tale's sick Jewish "hero" would actually die... Surely, Kassovitz is speaking to the French state here, reminding it that no matter how long it has preserved an aura of permanence, no one knows what will happen in the "end?"

Page 54:

You write of human telephonic practice as retaining traces of the paradigm of the face-to-face conversation. But curiously, the format we have chosen—long entries with long interruptions—makes this much more like an epistolary interrogation than an e-mail exchange, and in almost no way does it model on face-to-face presence. Even less is our format like traditional Talmud study, in which, as my brother once put it, time stops, so that "a question asked in the sixteenth century is answered in the eleventh." Fine, this seems to imply that Talmud Torah makes sense in an Einsteinian universe, but how does it articulate with your notion of "historical" time, and what purchase do we have from the answer to this question?

Page 64:

Again on the Jabès quote, and here, as at other points, we approach the risky limits of this odd genre of fiction, since "you," the reader not-yet-named (not only Martin, I am confident, still) may have tired of gnawing on this particular bone. I can look again, but I think a non-contextual reading is entirely called for here. I realize now that I had always read the "I was" as the default situation; it would almost have to be read as "when you were silent, I was" or, more pointedly, perhaps "when you are silent, I was" (a curious form of relation between two subjects in, or at, two times or at least two tenses). Or, and also, "I was" means "I was only potential" and when "you speak" "I am actual." This could easily mean "I am actual" because you invoke me, you speak of me, you speak of the things that moved me and of which I spoke; or it could also mean, conversely (but I think not inconsistently with what Benveniste writes, and quite likely you are suggesting this as well if not in so many terms): when you address me I become actual. This would not require a dead ego; but I wonder whether it could in any case *include* a dead ego?

Page 66:

"*If humanity becomes extinct… we will be gone as if we had never been*:" But, for all your appropriate reluctance to indulge too much in language games, there is a distinction that makes a difference between "as if we had never been" (an entirely predictable if hardly imaginable future state) and "we never were." The latter is *not* a possible outcome for us in the historical future, I think. The difference is expressed by Benjamin's observation that when we speak of something that is "unforgettable," this is not so much a hortatory insistence on its importance for human memory as an assertion that it has a place in God's memory. Similarly (?) there is something about the inevitability of our having been that makes us aspire to the status of the best species we could possibly have been. For now, we do that, not so much by predicting the future as, through our discipline of predicting the future, trying to help make it possible. Welcoming the future stranger.

Page 69:

Therefore, if "the future... prediction is infuriatingly difficult to make," perhaps we need to understand a bit better why that difficulty infuriates us. It shouldn't; it should make us humble. If the present were not accompanied by such infinite misery unto death that seems inexorably emblematic of our now most likely futures, I would say that the very difficulty of predicting the future should if anything make us laugh. It is wrong, of course, to laugh too much at our neighbor's funeral.

"*table of contents*:" By the time I read your thln_004, I had virtually no memory of anything like a "list" of topics. In fact there are two, yours at thln_002 and mine at thln_001. By now I think we have touched on most of the items in your list, certainly in no way systematic enough that we might extract a table of contents! Perhaps we have not mentioned two.

As to "looking at other conclusions from linguistics that might affect a post-marketplace view of human relations," perhaps we might start there at some unpredictable point in the future. (From both the commentary form to which I have been driven here, and your own recourse to quite everyday notions of past, present and future at page 69, I begin to sense that this particular exchange is drawing toward a provisional ending.)

In response to your proposal that we discuss "[t]he near-simultaneous emergence of scientific claims of imminent climatic catastrophe, apocalyptic millenarianism among fundamentalist Jews and Christians, and suicide terrorism—is Death the new Life?" (and also in response to my own initial reference to Ralph Bakshi's movies), I offer the following anecdote:

As you know, Jonah's been attending the intensive summer Yiddish program at YIVO. Yesterday afternoon I'd been planning to pick him up right after class at 3:00 and take him to New Jersey to visit my mother. He called in the morning to explain he was going to spend the day shooting a music video instead, and I walked over to visit him on the "set." He explained that he'd been walking down the sidewalk on his way to class and, when stopped to find out what was going on, someone approached him to ask if he'd spend the day "playing a rabbi" in the video for a song about, as he says, "the end of the world." With his thin facial hair, a long black costume jacket, fake *payess* and big black hat, he looks like a *yeshiva bokher* on the Yiddish stage: but he convincingly looks like that. Evidently in the crowd scene, he and someone else dressed as a Muslim are supposed to be praying together. I reminded him of the "praying rabbis" scene in Bakshi's *Wizards*, which I described above in *Time and Human Language Now*. Bakshi made his film, of course, before the end of the world became a fashionable theme (though after David Bowie's song "Five Years"). Now the theme of "the end of the world" seems to teeter on the verge of being passé. (God reminiscing about when those funny people God created worried about the end of their world.)

And, as to my own proposed list of topics, two can be alluded to briefly here:

Item 4: "*If it* [language] *stopped for a generation, the whole thing would be lost.*" We are, at any rate, keeping it going, in the present. As to the future, what will have been, will have been.

Item 5: My concerns about the inevitability of egotistic motives "infecting" such a purely speculative effort at this. Solved; now that, for the most part, this exchange *has been*, it still doesn't make me feel especially smart (so much is missed, so many wheels are reinvented!), let alone confident that others will be impressed by all this, but it's been fun for the most part.

Evolutionary Postscript

The word "evolution" appears significantly but without elaboration in thln_004 (for example, at page 44, "[t]he evolution parameter is called the historical time...") One of the vital thought-tasks for which our species has precious little time is the articulation of its evolution (self-directed only to a given extent) at various scales: its evolution in the broadest senses as part of what you call "historical time;" its biogenetic evolution; its cultural evolution. The last, of course, is part and parcel of the material universe and both of the latter, of course, are thoroughly encompassed within historical time. I am speaking now of different senses of the word "evolution," not of different "things." What (to suggest, by way of another possible re-starting point) lessons for personal action do we draw from the recognition that our human chronology, our past, present and future, all of our potential "having been" is evolutionary, neither fated nor doomed nor arbitrary product of grace? If I am the product of evolution, what is my product to be? Should I suffer to reduce my carbon footprint, whether or not anyone else does? What kind of statement is that, what kind of act? Should we (you and I, for example) humbly but otherwise blithely accept our relative good placement as the scope of environments that sustain human life (and human numbers) shrinks?

I found compelling, just a few years ago, that (with phenomena such as the second election of George W. Bush, or the "intelligent design" debates) the phrase "evolution lost." It evoked in my mind both "this view of life" as something precious that we no longer have or at least have placed at moral risk, and, insofar as extinction and thus an end at last to the evolution of our species seemed much more plausible, the notion of a contest in which the very process of evolution itself had failed. The latter at least was a fallacy, for as Peter J. Richerson and Robert Boyd lucently point out in their recent book *Not By Genes Alone*, that a cultural pattern may be maladaptive (leading toward extinction rather than species success) hardly means it is not a product of evolution.

In evolutionary terms, the phrase I was looking for (though much less evocative) was doubtless something more like "adaptation lost." When we say "adaptive," we refer to that which fosters the likelihood of reproduction. Moreover, while we know that extinction is part of evolution, we tend to casually associate evolutionary success with a progression from past to future (hence the mild astonishment of a younger anthropologist colleague at my assertion that I take an evolutionary but not a progressive perspective). We cannot reproduce ourselves in the past—or can we? If you are right that "the past represents the events we can possibly have observed and recorded in memory," then it is certainly true at least that our capacities to observe and record can grow and in *that* sense at least the past expands toward the future. As Richerson and Boyd predict, "[m]ore surprises in both past and future climates are virtually a certainty."

thin_006 (Martin)

A curious feature of physical theory is that many basic results can be found by apparently unrelated methods or arguments. For example, the sounds produced by a musical instrument can be described by solving the equations associated with a detailed model of vibrations on a string or in a hollow cavity, and the same result is obtained by naively multiplying and dividing the physical parameters available in the problem until a quantity emerges that represents pitch. For some, this confluence of approaches—many paths to the Buddha, one might be tempted to say—is evidence of an underlying holistic reality that unifies apparently distinct methods as connected facets of a deeper theory. On the other hand, careful scientists must also consider that such coincidence may possibly be the telltale sign of self-referential and rigged (or conspiratorial) circularity. So, for example, when we find that our interpretation of history makes equal sense going forward and backward, we must ask ourselves whether this agreement is a check on our thinking—like adding up a restaurant bill in reverse order—or have we engineered a universe in which nothing can contradict our prejudices.

These thoughts come to mind as I consider that the questions you ask do follow naturally from the previous section, and yet invite me to close this part of our discussion on precisely the path I am predisposed to follow. Is it possible, Jonathan, that your law professors taught you well in the art of the leading question? Have years of teaching taught me to treat questions as just another opportunity to continue making my original point? Or is this convergence part of what we call language?

In my previous contribution I tried to excuse my long excursion into the physics of time as shaped by a pair of related impulses—first, an uncontrollable desire, common among teachers, to propagate the insights drawn from years of study and share the excitement that understanding can generate, and second, an "irresistible anxiety" that if I do not describe my ideas in sufficient detail, they will be misunderstood. Superficially, this secondary anxiety appears only to sharpen the primary narcissism, without which teachers would be unable to push ideas and interpretations for a living, but my concern here is not to label any variation on my understanding of physics as wrong. Although I had not fully articulated my concerns to myself while writing, my discussion of time was influenced by a desire to avoid three specific misreadings.

My first concern was to approach the subject in a way that would be recognizable by working physicists, not only because translating the language of physics and mathematics into English prose is always difficult, but specifically because the topic is outside the mainstream of physics education. Although the parameter I call historical time appears in equations familiar to second or third year physics students, little attention is generally paid to its underlying significance or its wider possibilities; most presentations of electromagnetism, gravitation, cosmology, and elementary particle theory problematically lump the historical time (string theory has two such objects) together with a different quantity known as proper time. Fearing that an abbreviated discussion would leave too few points of connection for physicists, and with no small fear of being branded a heretic, I found myself impelled to inflation.

A second occasion of disquiet is the complexity of the essential goal—introducing a highly abstract and technical aspect of contemporary physics in a manner sufficiently comprehensible to non-specialists that it may be used as evocative metaphor in the wider context of human experience. The first part of this goal, translating the physics into English, is made difficult by the compactness and efficiency of its indigenous mathematical language, which naturally unpacks into irritatingly wordy prose that can obscure its own meaning. The second part, extracting from this language a useful vocabulary for the discussion of time in human experience, runs a contrary risk—the historic tendency to endow scientific ideas with exaggerated authority, in matters outside their natural context and domain of application. Social Darwinism and the mechanistic view imposed on the world by enlightenment thinkers, eager to duplicate the success of Newton's mechanics, have long been textbook examples of the perversion of scientific principle (a formal summary of causal relationships among highly abstracted representations of simple inanimate objects) into a crude interpretation of social behavior. Even today, despite Marx's ancient warning about the likely origin of "the ruling ideas," the present day temptation to reduce all human experience to microbiology and quantum mechanics is apparently immune to postmodern skepticism, even among many new age thinkers. But my borrowing from biological science, characterizing an idea as "immune" to skepticism or "resistant" to change, has no greater force than using the language of art to describe an experience as impressionistic or surreal. For this reason I repeatedly emphasized that discoveries regarding the temporal subtleties of elementary particle interactions may have the power to undermine the existing moral imperative to view time as one-dimensional, and may encourage a wider reconsideration of traditional and intuitive conceptions of time, but do not imply that people can or must behave like elementary particles, temporally or otherwise. Similarly, the randomness associated with quantum mechanics does not imply a scientific statement that our lives are random, or that humans may spontaneously tunnel from one part of the universe to another. Such phenomena may indeed be possible, but it will probably be some time before science can appropriately formulate these questions, let alone answer them. In this sense, it is entirely reasonable to state that in the world of Talmud, "A question asked in the sixteenth century is answered in the eleventh," asserting a kind of temporality familiar to us from the microscopic causality of elementary particles, but the statement stands or falls as an observation about Talmud, not on any purported scientific statement about causality.

In response to a related question, I do not apologize for science, nor do I see it as the prime culprit in the exaggeration of its importance. Science understands and lives by its own limitations—it seeks to find regularity in a limited domain of observable phenomena that are amenable to controlled and repeatable experimentation. The scientific method translates experimental observations into theory—explicitly reductionist models that replicate an abstraction of these phenomena and can be manipulated, in place of direct empirical observation, to study certain essential features of this abstraction. The "explanatory power" of the method—the extraordinary level of agreement between theory and experiment for whatever underlying reason—is unquestionable, as is our ability to exploit this power through technology. And yet the euphoria this power induces, and our continuing search for unifying simplification, can lead to a kind of tunnel vision. Just as children learning to speak attempt to reduce the scale of that daunting task by imposing regularity on irregular cases—"I goed" instead of "I went"—we seek to push the regularizing power of science beyond its proper domain of application, until we find ourselves thinking—consciously or not—that whatever is not clearly reducible to known science simply cannot be. Despite the broad variety of experiences that cannot be subject to controlled and repeatable experimentation, the success of the scientific method has encouraged a thoroughly unscientific proposition to grow up around it—a foundational conception of our universe as assembled entirely from pieces that can be completely understood by one or another reductionist model. In its extreme form, this conception outdoes the reductionism of the old mechanistic social theories by converting renaissance-era prescriptions for scientific model-building into a general framework for epistemology and ontology, until only experimentally verifiable experience may be legitimately discussed, and consideration of anything else is deemed superstition, magic, religion, supernatural, and ultimately the preoccupation of inferior minds. This scientism, which converts experience (in the words of *The Communist Manifesto*) to a "commodity, like every other article of commerce," serves to modernize our rituals for coping with fear of the unknown by replacing "superstitious" belief in supernatural events with an equally superstitious belief in a world devoid of super-natural events. Entire fields of scholarship devote them-selves to the criticism and deconstruction of this unsci-entific enterprise, and while scientists are active in the criticism of other varieties of public irrationality, their general failure—since Einstein's passing—to criticize scientism is often mistaken for assent. But to the disap-pointment of some philosophers of science, even theo-retical physics cannot progress under empiricist funda-mentalism, and physicists who regard themselves as thoroughgoing realists willingly accept the existence of microscopic objects, such as quarks, whose direct observation is thought to be impossible in principle. To be sure, evidence-based reasoning remains safe, even in the quantum regime; the claim that the existence of non-observables can be inferred from experiment is ultimately shorthand for the statement that these objects play an irreducible role in an empirically well-established theory. But despite the success of the scientific method in its natural domain of application, where is the evidence for the claim that "everything must have a logical explanation"? It seems self-evident that just as science cannot disprove a claim that has no scientific formulation, it cannot disqualify consideration of such claims. The meaning of this book is trivialized if it becomes necessary to evaluate the scientific truth or falsity of Jabès' claim, "You are silent, I was; you speak, I am." Moreover, Benveniste's analysis of personal pronouns makes the intersubjective argument that human language permits shared understanding through its access to inherently subjective, non-empiri-cal experience. This is not to advocate any program of anti-rationalism, but to allow for the coexistence of that which can be demonstrated by evidence-based reasoning and that which cannot, without reducing either to ridicule by insisting that it masquerade as the other.

The maximalist empiricism associated with Rudolph Carnap's logical positivism and B. F. Skinner's behaviorism are no longer in favor, but the extreme reductionism that forces all experience into the domain of observable, scientific phenomena continues today in the search for genes that "cause" love, poverty, and religion. Another curious notion—known among fabulists of artificial intelligence—is the proposal to accelerate evolution by uploading the "memory content" of a human brain to a robot that will replace the human so that "he" will experience the continuation of "his" life through this engineered medium. What proportion of a human body can be exchanged for manufactured hardware is not merely an ethical question—I am personally certain that if progressively replacing my body parts with robotic elements and finally swapping my brain with an information-processing device could produce a sentient being, the assembled system would nevertheless constitute a "him" and not provide "me" with a continuous and coherent experience of the transition.

Reductionist scientism distorts the significance of subjective experience by pretending to treat it scientifically, but a possibly more dangerous consequence of restricting legitimacy to empirical phenomena is the countervailing tendency to "elevate" inherently subjective experience to the status of scientific truth. I suffer no illusion that followers of "intelligent design" would stop camouflaging their faith as science if only evolutionists were more respectful of faith-based meaning systems alongside empirically demonstrable explanation, but acknowledging the distinction may help eliminate one source of confusion in the public discourse. Unfortunately, the greater motivation for these camouflage manoeuvres is not to achieve intellectual legitimacy, but rather to acquire legal force. Science and democracy have an underlying connection in their common domain of application to matters that are publicly observable, and so the promotion of private experience as shared, public, scientific knowledge becomes the key to its admissibility as the basis for law.

This connection of science and democracy leads to my third concern, which also addresses your question, "How is science something separate?" Although its domain of application is limited, scientific models are unquestionably successful at "explaining the world," meaning that a "well-established theory" provides answers to scientifically meaningful questions that do not deviate in a significant way from direct empirical observation. Thus, bearing in mind these limitations and all other necessary caveats, the predictions made by a well-established theory can be regarded as knowledge, with no less certainty than direct, shared experience. Because science and democracy deal in matters of public record, they share an interest in distinguishing public and private experience, and an inherent preference for evidence-based reasoning to faith and intuition as justifications for collective action. While my personal intuition is obviously a legitimate source of knowledge for me, and its unscientific foundations do not disqualify it as a basis for personal action, it is unacceptable, in any theory of democracy, to impose it in the public sphere without an empirical basis for public testing in accordance with scientific method. But in the daily political realities of our two countries, this distinction is frequently inverted, with matters of private experience regularly hyped as the factual basis for law, and well-established scientific results dismissed as "only a theory." This inversion is a feature of the cultural maladaptation you discuss—it is highly adaptive to the cohesion of particular social circumstances, but poorly adapted to long-term survival.

Unfortunately, the fundamentalist right has not been alone in attacking the preference for evidence-based reasoning as an example of undue privilege. Science is a collective human activity and by its nature, socially constructed, which undoubtedly influences, at the least, the questions it asks, the methods it develops, the arguments it accepts or rejects, the constructs it regards as fundamental and complete, and its style of presentation. Consequently, different scientists working from different assumptions may choose to perform different experiments and consequently obtain different results. But the claim heard in certain quarters, that science is merely evocative prose about the private interests of scientists as a cultural group, and that different scientists working with different assumptions can perform identical experiments and nevertheless obtain different results, is dangerously overstated. Since science defines success as agreement between theory and observation, it can offer no further argument for its own value, once its claim to empirical agreement is dismissed as a tautological consequence of its own belief system. So, the most that can be said in this regard is to wish a happy future to those lucky souls who will not be affected by climate change because that particular construction is not a feature of their lifeworld. This connects somehow to the slogan, "We don't have to predict the future; we just have to make it possible," which reminds me of an exchange from *Waiting for Godot*:

VLADIMIR: That passed the time.
ESTRAGON: It would have passed in any case.
VLADIMIR: Yes, but not so rapidly.
ESTRAGON: What do we do now?
VLADIMIR: I don't know.

My response to the Lausanne slogan is, "No action whatsoever is required of us to make the future possible—it will arrive in any case. But if we do not predict the future, it is likely that we ourselves will not participate." Again, I suffer no illusion that confused thinking is what brought humanity to the brink of extinction, and I continue to see material relationships as the nexus of collective experience and understanding. Accordingly, there is little point in offering formulas for a prescriptive social contract that will somehow, with a mighty hand and an outstretched arm, settle all outstanding issues in social theory, beginning with, "How do we agree on what we know, with reference to which assumptions and observations, and how do we get there from here?" I will be satisfied to help by undermining one source of political confusion, and in this effort, I wear a T-shirt with the slogan "Climate Change. It's only a fact." In writing about time, my concern was to avoid blurring the distinction between well-established theory, speculation, and metaphor, and yet feel free to move rapidly between these forms.

Several of your questions go to the heart of relativity as a principle of physics. In general, physics recognizes that observations are inherently particularistic, and only have meaning in relation to the observer's tools, methods, condition of motion, point of view, reporting, and so on, considerations referred to collectively as the observer's frame of reference. Although the reference frame is itself constructed from the very objects of physical study, careful use of operational definitions permits a usefully consistent set of shared meanings to be established and publicly shared, a primary function of language. In this spirit (meaning propensity, not spirituality), physical influence simply means a consistent pattern of phenomena amenable to controlled, repeatable, and publicly agreed-upon experiment, whether or not a corresponding theory exists. The goal of these definitions is to clearly distinguish the subjectivity of human experience, which can only partially be made public, from the particularity of the frame of reference—while observers in different frames will measure events differently, any two observers in the same frame will make essentially identical measurements, providing operational meaning to a notion of objectivity.

Principles, on the other hand, must hold for every collection of observations considered in relation to one another, regardless of reference frame. The principle of relativity states that when viewing the same event from different reference frames, the reported observations will differ, and no particular reference frame offers a privileged view. Nevertheless, the principle asserts that the differences are predictable and depend on measurable relationships among the frames of reference, so that certain mathematical combinations of observations are identical for all reference frames, and a full set of observations in one frame can be calculated from the observations in another frame. This statement of relativity is similar to the customary argument for relativism in the humanities, recognizing that truth depends on the observer's frame of reference, but differs in its concern with comparing and correlating the views of different observers when they share a unique object of examination.

To specify a reference frame in physics requires four axes, which can be thought of as measuring devices—three measuring sticks (rulers) and a clock, leaving aside speculation about additional dimensions. A dimension is any direction along which one can point a measuring device in order to measure some sense of separation (spatial or temporal) that cannot be measured or known by a different combination of measurements. As long as the measuring devices extend into all four dimensions, their particular orientation does not affect the ability to make measurements and relate these to measurements made with respect to differently oriented axes. So there is no excuse for a culture war in the fact that a box 40 inches high and 30 inches wide will be described as 30 inches high and 40 inches wide by an observer who has exchanged the "high"-axis and "wide"-axis. Similarly, relativity in space-time states that a pair of events observed in one frame as occurring simultaneously at distance of 30 inches may be observed in a different frame to occur sequentially (one after the other) at a distance of 29 inches. The events have not changed, but the observed spatial and temporal separations depend on the observer's frame of reference.

I had in mind precisely the analogies you mention to social phenomena when I criticized the reification of the Cartesian coordinate idea, its extension to the idea of empty space-time as an "arena" for physical events, and the related abstraction of forces that permeate this background arena. The physical viewpoint that emphasizes foundational quantities—reciprocal dyadic physical interactions that depend on their localized spatial and temporal separation, without reference to the "arena"—is indeed more compelling, both in physics and social theory, because by proceeding without reference to "background forces" that materialize from the "arena", it avoids the need to subsequently deconstruct those forces. Moreover the viewpoint seems closer to the dialectical approach of Hegel and Marx, in which "universal forces" are no more than shorthand for interactions among humans who participate in the creation of systems that in turn determine their lives, even systems that evolve into the Stalinist and Nazi regimes. Diamond's analysis is protected from the charge of moral relativism by a principle of moral relativity—events appear differently when viewed from different perspectives, but by considering in detail how and why the frames of reference differ, the divergent perceptions of the same underlying events can be correlated. Certainly the "lessons of history" most applicable to the future are those that address the problem of how actions that are recognized as atrocities from below (or from outside) appear to the perpetrators to be a perfectly reasonable response to existential conditions. Lewis Feuer, in *Einstein and the Generations of Science*, attributes to Einstein the following analogy: The heliocentric description of planets orbiting a stationary sun, as observed in the sun's reference frame, is no truer than the Ptolemaic description of the sun and planets orbiting a stationary earth, as observed in the earth's reference frame, but has the advantage of providing a considerably simpler model and clearer path to understanding. Similarly, Einstein argued, historical events as seen by an oppressed class are no truer than the perceptions of the oppressor, but the perspective of the oppressed provides a simpler and more transparent account. In the present reality, the perspective of those who may suffer the pecuniary consequences of reducing greenhouse gases can be similarly correlated with the perspective of a future generation of Floridians who, like today's besieged polar bears, will be confined to a diminishing land mass.

As I admitted earlier, the detailed consideration of how physical theory describes the microscopic evolution of space-time events is something of a narrow specialization, primarily intended to construct at a more coherent description of relativistic dynamics. Meanwhile, the various formulations lead to empirically indistinguishable results, and no well-established theory permitting specific, reliable predictions about such exotic questions as time travel or highly complex chronologies has been singled out. Consequently, the discussion of historical or chronological time versus coordinate time can only present the ingredients of a reasonable physical model. In this model, as you successfully grasped, the historical time specifies the chronological order of events as they unfold, and the specification of chronology is essentially equivalent to announcing a causal principle: no event can affect a chronologically prior event. Chronological order is therefore more fundamental than the concept of spatial and temporal location in space-time, which is ultimately a double abstraction, first from separation of events to Cartesian coordinates, and second from coordinates to the "empty arena" of physical interaction. When the words past and present refer to chronology, they describe non-overlapping physical environments, but when they refer to coordinate time, they describe a kind of separation between possibly interacting events at a given chronological moment. As the chronological time advances, one configuration of events, dispersed across spatial and temporal separations, evolves into a new configuration, producing a new space-time configuration at each chronological moment. Thus, while events may effectively interact over finite spatial and temporal separations, (at a given chronological moment, space and time "trail off" at some large separation from my frame of reference), the end of chronological time would complicate physical theory tremendously, and is essentially a question to which physics has no access.

The interplay of coordinate space and time, through the principle of relativity, suggests that just as an object can leave home at 9:00 am and return at 5:00 pm, so it can leave home at 9:00 am and return home at 9:00 am, at a later chronological time. The description of events moving to and fro in space while moving forward and backward in time depends dramatically on the coordinate time in the observer's frame of reference, because events are recorded in the order of their observation, not in the chronological order of their evolution. Essentially, each observer's clock imposes a particular perception of simultaneity on the surrounding environment, while the physically relevant causal "present" is knowable only from a posteriori analysis of causation. In the standard example, pair annihilation, an observer describes two event trajectories converging to a space-time point and then vanishing in a flash of light—a narrative that can be reinterpreted chronologically as the observer's private view of an object that proceeds first forward and then backward through coordinate time. While moving backward through coordinate time (according to this observer) the object produces events that the observer (recording events by the laboratory clock) records in the reverse order of their production, so that chronologically later events of the trajectory appear before the chronologically earlier events. Presumably, a second observer co-moving with the object will perceive the objects in the first observer's lab in an equally complicated way.

You pose a far more difficult question, and a matter of current interest in physics, in regard to the seemingly artificial distinction between the observer and the objects of experiment. Since all observers are made of objects that interact physically, it seems natural to view the process of observation as simply an interaction. And yet the making of records—the production of memory—is an irreversible process, a special kind of interaction whose analysis is a fundamental unsolved problem for physics. For example, many quantum systems can exist in a mixture of mutually exclusive states simultaneously, in a proportion that has probabilistic interpretation, and when two such systems interact, all possible states of one system interact with all possible states of the other, producing a system in a new mixture of mutually exclusive states. But when such systems are observed, they mysteriously "collapse" into one or another of their mutually exclusive states. In relativity, observations are distinguished from interactions in that the observer assembles a picture out of all chronological events, reordering them according to a particular laboratory clock. Physicists refer to the resulting trajectories—shorn of information about the underlying chronology of their evolution—as worldlines, representing the entire series of events that add up to a lifetime. Therefore, observation is different from other forms of interaction, and while there are many promising leads, there is no consensus among physicists how to approach this difference.

Given the large number of questions still unanswered for microscopic particles, any scientific consideration of such exotic questions as time travel or highly complex chronologies among macroscopic humans is essentially limited to what can be ruled out as illogical. For example, the conundrum presented in "Back to the

Future" involving time travel and revision of history with recognizable consequences for the present, requires a series of poorly defined assumptions: an infinite space-time arena made up of events trapped at their assigned time coordinates in eternal repetition, and an opposing mechanism that permits the spontaneous relocation of some events to different coordinates. Any alternative picture depends heavily on the particular model of interactions, but one possibility is that the events we call 1956 occurred at one chronological moment, were registered in memory, and then moved on to 1957, so that a current day visitor to the Southern California of 1956 would find nothing but empty space-time. Perhaps a reliable physical theory explaining how anti-particles can have arrived at future coordinate times— a precondition for their evolving to our earlier coordinate times in the well-accepted pair annihilation model— may one day shed light on these problems. In any case, any past events that contributed to my being must have chronologically preceded anything I do, and therefore are beyond my power to change.

A Clumsy Ending

You are certainly right to distinguish the characterization of human extinction by "as if we had never been" and not "we never were." We cannot change the chronological past, neither can we erase the historical record we leave behind—in fact the changes our behavior will have induced in earth's environment may be our most significant legacy. Put slightly differently, God will certainly remember us, but perhaps not remember us fondly.

Meanwhile, this exercise in pre-nostalgia is about to stop, and I find myself asking what were we thinking when we began? It was something about the miracle of human communication in language, the relationship of language to memory, time and useful predictions—the possibility that language could help us build a future that is wise enough not to exclude the likelihood of human survival from the index of leading economic indicators. With so many omissions from this conversation, and so many possibilities thrown into the air that never fell back into the discussion, I am left with the feeling that this book may join the pile of others I have promised myself to read one day, so that I can find out what it's about. If only there were more time. And this is precisely the unanswered question—can that lament be communicated in human language, and translated into a set of relationships that allows us to bring it about? Time itself is in no apparent danger of stopping, but present indications suggest that several higher life forms on this planet are about to be silenced in mid-sentence, leaving billions of messy narratives with no meaningful conclusion. ■

Also available from Prickly Paradigm Press:

continued